CHANGE IS GOOD

True Stories from the Austin Area

Table of Contents

ACKNOWLEDGEMENTS

I would like to thank Kermit Bell and Sam Russo for their vision for this book and for their hard work in making it a reality. To the people of GTaustin, thank you for your boldness and vulnerability in sharing your personal stories.

This book would not have been published without the amazing efforts of our project manager and editor, Debbie Maxwell Allen. Her untiring resolve pushed this project forward and turned it into a stunning victory. Thank you for your great fortitude and diligence. Deep thanks to our incredible editor in chief, Michelle Cuthrell, and executive editor, Jen Genovesi, for all the amazing work they do. I would also like to thank our invaluable proofreader, Melody Davis, for the focus and energy she puts into perfecting our words.

Lastly, I want to extend our gratitude to the creative and very talented Michael Bell, Christopher Bell and Ariana Randle, who designed the beautiful cover for *Change Is Good: True Stories from the Austin Area.*

Daren Lindley
President and CEO
Good Catch Publishing

The book you are about to read
is a compilation of authentic life stories.
The facts are true, and the events are real.
These storytellers have dealt with crisis, tragedy, abuse
and neglect and have shared their most private moments,
mess-ups and hang-ups in order for others to learn and
grow from them. In order to protect the identities of those
involved in their pasts, the names and details of some
storytellers have been withheld or changed.

INTRODUCTION

Some of the happiest and most contented people I know have overcome great difficulties finding a way to keep circumstances from defining their life. I remember looking into the hopeful eyes of children living in difficult circumstances and wondering, *At what point will their life experience cause their hopes and dreams about their future to begin to fade?*

Anyone who has lived more than a couple of decades soon realizes that life rarely turns out as you imagined. In addition, there will be resistance, roadblocks, crises and plenty of other things that can add to the disappointment in life.

You hold in your hand eight true stories of real people who have overcome all that life could throw at them. They found a way to move beyond huge obstacles in order to bring about change in their lives.

Your life really can change. It is possible to become a new person. Whether you've been beaten by abuse, broken promises, shattered dreams or suffocating addictions, the resounding answer is, "Yes! You can become a new person." The potential to break free from gloom and into a bright future awaits.

Expect inspiration, hope and transformation! As you walk with these real people from right here in Austin through the pages of this book, you will not only find riveting accounts of their hardships, you will learn the secrets that brought about their breakthroughs. These people are no longer living in the shadows of yesterday; they are thriving with a sense of mission and purpose *today.* May these stories inspire you to do the same.

Change is good!

Kermit Bell

TWO WORLDS COLLIDE
The Story of Luke and Amanda
Written by Karen Koczwara

What happened to me?

I glanced down, gasping in horror at the pool of blood under my bottom. I felt myself hemorrhaging, and the intense pain made me gasp. My clothes were off, my memories of the night before all a blur.

The guys in the bar! That drink! It's the last thing I remember. Did they ... rape me?

Groggily, I reached for the phone next to the bed and dialed the operator for help. Next, I began frantically searching for my clothes.

Tell me this is all a nightmare. Tell me this did not happen.

My heart raced as I yanked on my clothes and stumbled out of the room.

This is bad — really bad.

I need help, now!

❧❧❧

Amanda

When I was 7 years old, doctors diagnosed me with type 1 diabetes. Instead of being preoccupied with which doll to play with or what flavor ice cream to eat, I worried about doctor visits, blood sugar woes and daily shots. My mother took me regularly to an endocrinologist, where he performed lots of tests and used fancy words I could hardly pronounce. Overnight, my world changed. I was forced to grow up, to monitor every bite I took. At school, my classmates stared while I ate my mid-morning snack, and I grew embarrassed. How could I explain my disease when I hardly understood it myself?

My father's alcoholism and infidelity took a toll on my parents' marriage, and when I turned 8, they divorced. The following year, I moved with my mother from our home in Texas to Las Vegas, where her two sisters lived. My father remained in Texas and married the woman he'd cheated on my mother with. I tried to settle into my new school but found it difficult. My school in the small Texas town we'd lived in had just 200 kids. So many more kids attended my new school. I felt lost in the crowd, an outsider who did not belong.

A few years later I went to live with my father in Texas for a year and a half, but I didn't feel welcome in his home. I thought my stepsisters and stepmother did not treat me well and often suspected they talked about me behind my back. It seemed my father had made a new life for himself, and I no longer had a place in that life. I returned to Vegas, back to an unstable environment. Life felt lonely and dull. It felt like something was missing, and I couldn't find it.

By age 13, I began using drugs, smoking cigarettes and drinking alcohol. I sought out older friends, hanging out with people nearly twice my age. My mother enrolled me in high school, but I hated it just as much as I'd loathed middle school. I grew depressed, no longer interested in my studies or any other positive activities. My mother sent me back to Texas for a while to live with my father. As my apathy worsened, my father took notice and hospitalized me for depression.

I spent nearly three weeks in a mental ward, surrounded by kids who struggled with drugs, eating disorders and other behavioral problems. The doctors put me on antidepressants and worked on keeping my blood sugar under control. They mandated a strict schedule and kept us locked up at all times. I felt like a prisoner, trapped in rooms with bare white walls. At last, they released me and sent me on my way. But my depression continued.

At 15, I realized I'd have to take care of myself. My mother developed a bad gambling habit, often disappearing to the casinos for days at a time. She held various jobs at medical clinics, doing medical billing and other front office work. On Fridays, she cashed her paycheck during lunchtime, then headed for the casinos, often not returning home until late Sunday night. My mother gambled all our money away, going back and forth between two boyfriends and changing living situations and jobs several times.

I fended for myself, scraping together whatever I could find in the fridge. I remember making many egg sandwiches in the microwave, as that was sometimes the only food in the house. At that young age, I became like the parent in our relationship, worrying about my mother's unhealthy habits as they increased. I began working two jobs to pay the bills and keep food in the fridge. My resentment grew as my mother's irresponsible behavior continued. Teenage girls were supposed to go shopping at the mall with their friends, discuss lip gloss colors, giggle about cute boys and go to the movies. They were not supposed to work two jobs to keep a roof over their heads.

My mother continued her disappearing act, leaving for days at a time. When I needed to find her, I picked up the phone and called every casino in Vegas to have her paged. One day, I could not take it any longer. I'd reached my breaking point. When she finally came home, I lashed out at her like I never had before.

"I'm sick of this!" I cried. "You leave me alone for days at a time and expect me to take care of everything around here. Well, I'm done! I'm just a kid! You're supposed to be a mother, but you're too busy gambling our money away all the time!"

"Don't you talk to me that way," my mother snapped back.

"Well, I'm tired of this! It's getting really old! Why don't you grow up!" I began throwing things around the room, completely enraged.

"Stop it, Amanda! Just stop it! You're out of control!" she screamed. "If you don't knock it off, I'm going to call the cops!"

"Fine!"

I continued storming around the apartment, hurling anything I could get my hands on. At last, I marched into the bathroom, slammed the door and locked it. I leaned against the wall, fighting back tears, my heart pounding in my chest. *I'm so sick of living this way! Why can't she see what she's doing?*

A few minutes later, I heard a knock at the door. "Amanda, we need to talk to you."

Crap. She really called the cops. I slowly opened the door. "Yeah?" I stared the cop in the eye.

"Your mother called and said you were out of control. Can we talk to you for a minute?"

I stepped out into the hall. The cop told me he'd haul me away if I did not calm down. After he left, I grabbed my things and left. "I'm going to stay with my boyfriend," I told my mother. "I'm done here."

I moved in with my boyfriend, who was attending the University of Las Vegas. We had two other roommates, and I found myself feeling settled and living a responsible life, taking vacations, making good decisions. Yet I still struggled with depression.

When I turned 19, we broke up, and I found a place of my own.

My mother called, needing a place to stay. "Can I move in with you?" she asked. "I'm down and out."

I reluctantly agreed to let her move in. I hoped she might contribute toward covering some of the expenses, but instead, she continued gambling her paychecks away.

"I see nothing's changed, Mom," I said with a sigh.

"You can't keep staying here, living like this. I'm trying to take care of myself. I can't take care of both of us."

The cycle had gotten old. My mother should have been my support system in this crazy city, yet I could not count on her.

I continued with my life, dating different guys, starting to go out to clubs and working full time. Though I was underage, I never had trouble getting in the door of the clubs. One of my friends was sleeping with the bouncer of a club, so he let us in without question. I began drinking and trying different drugs, living the fast life on the Las Vegas strip. I landed a job working at an adult video store, selling pornographic material. The drunken nights blurred into hazy days. I was out to have a good time.

At 20, I discovered I was pregnant.

At first, I contemplated keeping the baby. But I knew I could not raise a child with my boyfriend. He was physically abusive and had cheated on me several times. We had repeatedly broken up and gotten back together. If we did not have a stable relationship, how could we bring a baby into the mix?

My mother and my friends encouraged me to have an abortion. "You're too young," they said. "You can't raise a baby on your own."

They're right. I scheduled an abortion. When the day arrived, I walked through the doors of the clinic, feeling very afraid. When the technician performed the ultrasound, I turned my head away so I couldn't see anything. The procedure turned out to be more painful than I'd imagined. When it was over, I stumbled into the parking lot and threw up.

Life felt meaningless, empty and confusing. I'd tried finding happiness in every way I could — alcohol, men, drugs, having a good time. But nothing really worked. At the end of the day, I was still without purpose. I felt homesick, as though I was missing something I could not put my finger on. I thought there might be a God, but I couldn't imagine what he'd want with me if he did exist. I kept on searching, hoping something, someday, might make sense. I felt like I was in a mental battle.

When I was 22, my mother moved back to Texas, settling north of Dallas. I remained in Las Vegas and continued casually dating a guy I'd met at a casino after a Christmas party. Not long after we began hanging out, I discovered I was pregnant. This time, I chose to keep the baby.

When my boyfriend learned of my pregnancy, he decided he wanted nothing to do with me. When I was seven months along, he kicked me out of his apartment. I stayed in my car for a couple days, then moved in with a friend.

My pregnancy proved difficult because of my diabetes. Toward the end, the doctors ordered bed rest. Unable to work, I lay on my friend's couch, bored and lonely, counting the days until the baby's arrival. Three weeks before my due date, doctors induced labor due to my low amniotic fluid. Ready or not, I was about to have a baby.

Thirty minutes before I pushed and delivered the

baby, my father called with bad news. "Your grandfather died," he said.

The timing felt like it could not have been worse. At once, both spectrums of life collided, one life leaving this world as another entered it. My daughter was born healthy and beautiful, and I named her Jenna. I took her home, suddenly daunted by fear. *How am I supposed to raise this baby on my own? What if something happens to her? How am I supposed to protect her from all this junk in the world, especially living in Las Vegas?*

Jenna cried incessantly. I grew more depressed, watching my friends go out and have fun while I stayed home to soothe a fussy baby. One day, her crying became especially loud. The cops showed up at my door to tell me a neighbor had complained about the noise.

"Is everything okay?" they asked.

I burst into tears. "I don't know what's wrong with her. I've tried everything!" I cried.

"She might have gas," they said.

The cops left, and I plopped onto the couch with my gassy, uncontrollable baby. *What am I going to do? My mother's in Texas now. I have no money and no help. I can't stay in Vegas, trying to raise this baby on my own.*

When Jenna turned 3 months old, I decided to return to Texas. I moved in with my father. I remained anxious for my daughter's future and continued searching for something I could not identify. *Maybe I should go to church,* I decided. I had only attended church a handful of times with my grandmother growing up, and I hadn't thought about going in years. But as a new mother, I thought perhaps it might be a good idea. I needed something positive for my daughter.

I showed up at a little church one Sunday morning and settled into the pew. The preacher talked about how having a child out of wedlock was a sin, and I squirmed in my seat. *That certainly wasn't the message I was hoping to hear today. If this is what church and Christianity is all about, I don't think I want anything to do with it.*

I decided not to go back.

Before long, I met a new guy, Eric. We moved to Austin together, and I became pregnant again. I had another little girl, Sarah. Eric and I married two years later, and his brother secured him some contract work in Iraq. We decided I'd move to Greece to be near him while he worked.

I asked my mother to come with us, hoping she could help me with the girls. We packed our things and headed overseas, prepared for a new adventure. I grew excited as we touched down on the island of Crete, the place we'd be living.

Our gorgeous new home included a pool overlooking the Mediterranean Sea. Sandy beaches lay just miles from us. The scene was picture-perfect in every way. *I can't believe I get to live here. This is a dream.*

But the dream quickly turned into a nightmare. I learned my husband was having an affair with someone at work. I confronted him and asked for a divorce, but he refused. Sick over what he'd done, I took the girls and returned to the United States on my own. Eric remained in Iraq.

Realizing my marriage was over, I decided to try online dating. I saw a cute guy, Luke, on a social media site and decided to message him. I didn't hear back from him for a couple weeks. At last, he wrote me back, and we agreed to meet. We went out for a drink one night and hit it off. We made the rounds at a couple neighborhood bars, and everyone stopped to say hello to him.

"You know everyone around here," I told Luke, laughing. *This guy is even cuter in person. I really like him.*

Luke and I began dating from that moment on. Little did we know the trials and joys that awaited us just around the corner.

⮞⮞⮞

Luke

As a newborn, I was given up for adoption. After a year with a loving foster family, my adoption became official, and a few years later, my parents adopted my sister Chrissy. My father worked for the city of Austin, while my mother held a job as a registered nurse. As a tight-knit family, we enjoyed trips to New Mexico every Christmas to visit my grandmother, as well as other family outings. My mother made special home-cooked meals nearly every night, and both parents showered me and my sister with love and affection. Church played an active role in our lives as well, and we attended services together each Sunday.

From an early age, I struggled in school. The doctors diagnosed me with ADD and prescribed Ritalin. At age 5, I began playing soccer and thoroughly enjoyed the sport. I also participated in several school plays, which I liked, too. But my studies did not come easily for me, and my teachers put me in special classes with other learning-challenged students. I played the flute in middle school and enjoyed that, but my classmates began to pick on me. I felt different and hated being on medication. In the eighth grade, I put my foot down and told my pediatrician I did not want to take pills anymore.

"I'm done!" I said emphatically.

My parents, though frustrated, agreed to let me stop taking my meds. They enrolled me in honors algebra, as well as other mainstream classes. I kept up with soccer, as well as tennis, basketball and school band. For the first time in years, I felt like a normal kid.

I enjoyed attending GTaustin and loved helping out with the younger kids' classrooms. I attended youth group, youth camps and other church-centered activities. The leaders read Bible stories and talked about a relationship with God, explaining that we could spend eternity in heaven with him if we made a decision to follow him with our lives. At 13, I prayed, inviting God into my heart and life and confessing the wrong things I'd done. It seemed like a good decision — my parents had prayed that prayer and encouraged me to do the same.

Though church had always been more of a social outlet for me, I decided it couldn't hurt to start praying and reading my Bible.

I continued going to church, but at 15, my interest waned. I stopped thinking about God and started thinking more about having a good time. At 16, I began hanging out with an older guy in the neighborhood. He offered me a beer, and I liked it well enough and began drinking here and there. Next, I tried weed. It didn't affect me much, but it was easier to get our hands on pot than booze, so I began smoking it regularly. I stopped going to church regularly, much to my parents' dismay. Next, I started taking pills, popping a few Xanax here and there. I enjoyed the quick high the drugs offered. Soon, I began living a wild, partying life, and the boy of my youth disappeared.

Just before turning 17, I went out with my friends one night and got high. We spent the next day partying and taking pills. I tripped and fell and cut my hand. But instead of going to the emergency room, I simply wound some medical tape around it and went on. After being gone three days, I finally wandered back home, high, bloody, shirtless and out of my mind.

"Where have you been? And what on earth is wrong with you?" My father met me in the yard, his eyes wide with concern over my absence and how unruly I looked.

Too high to hold a conversation, I stumbled inside. My father found 15 Xanax pills in my pocket and demanded answers. "We're really worried about you, Luke. You can't go on like this. You need help."

My parents found a faith-based rehab program called Victory House. "Son, if you are going to live in our house, you need to go to this place and get better," they insisted. I went to Victory House and stayed there for the next 11 and a half months. The time proved life-changing. The leaders provided daily structure and talked to us about God. I spent a great deal of time reading the Bible, immersing myself in the passages. For the first time in my life, I developed a true excitement about God. I had sat in church my whole life, listening to the songs, praying the prayers and hearing the stories. I had even invited God to be an active part of my life when I was 13. But I had never understood what it meant to really live for God, to pursue him on a daily basis. I finally understood that living a life of faith was not just about memorizing a bunch of Bible verses. It was about living out those verses, about talking to God as I went through the hardships of life. I believed he wanted the best possible life for me, one filled with peace and joy. And I believed I could experience that, and more, by following him. But I could not have it both ways. If I continued using drugs, drinking and trying to run my own life, I would surely wind up messed up again.

I don't want that, God, I prayed. *I know I've made some bad choices. But when I leave this place, I really want to be different. I want to live for you.*

My parents had planned a trip to Cancun, and I wanted to go with them. The leaders at Victory insisted I stay longer, but I decided to leave. *I'm a different person now. I have a strong faith in God. I feel physically and emotionally stronger. This place has served its purpose. I'm ready to go.*

I left the center and went to Mexico with my parents. Three days into the trip, when the guy at the pool offered me a drink, I didn't hesitate to say yes. *I guess age doesn't matter here in Mexico. That's cool.* I had a few drinks, thinking it was no big deal.

My parents let me move home, and I returned to youth group, trying to make better choices. The youth leaders, ever gracious, offered me a job doing maintenance around the church, and I happily accepted the position. I stayed on the straight path for the next few months, attending church regularly and trying to follow God. But soon, I began smoking weed and drinking again, falling back into my old ways.

One evening, I remembered the spare keys I'd made for the church. I snuck out and let myself into the church. I began rummaging through the youth administration building and found a money box in the closet. Inside, I discovered $200. Without thinking twice, I took the money and stuffed it in my pocket. *The church won't miss it,* I reasoned.

The next day, the youth pastor called me into his office, his eyes somber as I sat down. "We have an issue, and we know it's you," he said without mincing words. "There is money missing from the youth building. Do you know anything about it?"

I gulped hard and then broke down crying. "Yes, I took it," I confessed.

The youth leaders showed me the utmost compassion. "We can press charges, or you can agree to go to Teen Challenge," they said. "It's your choice."

I agreed to attend Teen Challenge, another faith-based program for teens and adults struggling with addiction. The next day, one of the church staff offered to drive me five hours to the Teen Challenge ranch in East Texas. I walked into the place, not knowing what to expect.

Over the next few months, I met people from all walks of life. Some had drug and criminal backgrounds, others came because of other addictions and struggles. As at Victory, Teen Challenge offered structure, support and a faith-based curriculum. I became immersed in my Bible, memorizing whole books of the Bible at a time. I grew excited about God again, ready to get my life back on track. *This time, I'm changing for good. I'm not going back to my old ways.*

Over the holidays, I went back home to visit my family. I hung out with an old friend, his girlfriend and the girlfriend's friend. She was one of the hottest girls I'd ever seen. When they began drinking, I passed, priding myself on staying sober. They ended up getting wasted, and though I did not, I hooked up with the girl I'd just met.

I returned to Teen Challenge but could not stop thinking about the girl. After just three days, I decided to leave to be with her. My leaders tried to talk me out of my hasty decision.

"Please don't leave," they urged me. "You are not ready yet."

But I didn't care. The girl captivated me, and I'd fallen under her spell. I went to the Greyhound bus station and headed home. My parents were not happy about my decision. I began drinking and smoking weed again, slipping right back into my old habits. I didn't end up with the girl I'd slept with, but I moved in with another girl I'd dated. I began doing harder drugs, like Ecstasy.

One night, we threw a party, and everyone took some Ecstasy. My girlfriend began overdosing in our bedroom, and everyone panicked and left. I raced to her side and found her stiff on the bed. High from taking the drug myself, I threw her in the car and drove her to the hospital. Her near-lifeless body felt like dead weight in my arms as I rushed into the emergency room and called for help. Sure she was going to die, I called her mother to deliver the terrible news. The doctors revived her, but the incident remained imprinted in my mind — a nightmare I could not forget.

The next few years were a blur of drugs and alcohol, dark nights and fuzzy days.

In 2003, I moved to Philadelphia with an ex-girlfriend. We hoped living by her parents might allow us to work things out. But instead, our relationship only worsened. Bored and lonely, I began drinking even more excessively.

After a brief six months, I realized Philadelphia was not working for me. My girlfriend and I broke up, and I returned to Austin. I moved in with a buddy who was a major in the Air Force. With a Ph.D. and a master's degree, he seemed to have it all, including money and success. But I soon learned he was a functioning addict, playing the role of a good, upstanding guy. He introduced me to cocaine, and I found a new love. Coke was like nothing I'd ever experienced before. While high on coke, I felt like I was flying. It seemed I could do anything, and I found it exhilarating. The drug sucked me in.

I got arrested a few times on misdemeanor charges, including unlawful carrying of a firearm after stealing my father's pistol. One night, after drinking and driving, the cops arrested me and slapped me with a DUI. I spent time in and out of jail, drinking and snorting cocaine in between stints. I managed to keep a job and a car, but the rest of my life unraveled. Cocaine ruled my life, and I couldn't wait for the next fix. The kid who'd walked out of Teen Challenge, having memorized books of the Bible, seemed long gone. The dark world of drugs and booze had sucked me in, convincing me I did not need God, church or anything else. I had hurt my parents terribly, but I no longer cared. I just wanted to have a good time and live in the moment. I'd worry about tomorrow later.

One day, I received a MySpace message from a pretty girl, Amanda. She mentioned loving to paint and told me she'd recently gotten into artistic modeling. *Wow, this girl seems too good to be true. Is she even real?* I ignored her message, convinced she must be fake. I'd had several bad experiences dating girls I'd met online and didn't want to get hurt again. But after two weeks, I wrote Amanda back and gave her a chance. We decided to go out for a drink. Within no time, our two worlds merged, our painful pasts silently steering us in dangerous directions as we moved forward together. We were in for the ride of a lifetime, neither of us predicting the roller coaster ahead.

ॐॐॐ

Amanda

After dating a short time, my girls and I moved in with Luke. My husband refused to sign the divorce papers, making my life difficult. I had found happiness with Luke, however, convinced he was the one for me. I learned he had a cocaine problem, and at first, I didn't like that.

"Please don't do that stuff around me," I begged him. I had not used cocaine for years and did not want to be around it. But after hanging out with Luke and his friends, I began to feel left out. Finally, I changed my mind and asked him if I could try it again, too. It quickly sucked me in. When high, I felt on top of the world. I stayed up for long periods of time, convinced I was invincible. To come down, I took Benadryl, Nyquil, Xanax or any other downer I could find. Before long, Luke lost his job because he could not function at work, and we began fighting regularly. One day, I checked his cell phone and learned he was still talking with another girl. I became enraged.

"How could you do this to me? I thought you were done with her!" I cried.

I moved out of the house for a couple days but then went back. We tried to work things out, but the fighting and drug use only worsened. Luke continued cheating on me, once leaving on a three-week binge and moving in with another girl. Fed up, I decided to move to North Texas to be with my mother. Luke called me often, begging me to come home.

"I can't live without you, Amanda," he said. "Please come back."

I relented and moved back in with him. Not long after, I learned I was pregnant. My heart sank, as did Luke's. This was not part of the plan. How could two people in such a dysfunctional relationship possibly raise a child together? It was hard enough raising my two girls in our rocky world.

"Let's have this baby and try to work things out," Luke suggested. "I think they offer free counseling at GTaustin, where I used to go."

I shrugged. "I guess it couldn't hurt."

Luke and I attended a couple of counseling sessions at his old church, and it helped a little. When our son, little Luke, entered the world, we both instantly fell in love with our tiny boy. But our happily ever after had not arrived yet. I still did not trust Luke, and we continued fighting and doing cocaine. I was fully addicted to the drug and lived for my next high. It brought excitement to our otherwise mundane life.

One day, when little Luke was just a few months old, I had a drink. I had been up for more than a day, high on coke, and hadn't slept a wink. As I held the baby in my lap, Luke, also high, reached over and slapped me. Infuriated, I posted about his behavior on Facebook. I didn't think much of it after that, but a week later, Child Protective Services showed up at our doorstep.

"We'd like to speak with you," said a woman.

CPS opened a case on us and began monitoring our every move. They did not take our children away but assured us they'd be watching us closely.

Instead of cleaning up our lives, we continued doing cocaine and fighting. The dark, abusive cycle continued. I loved Luke, and I knew he loved me, but we were too high most of the time to think straight.

Could we keep going on this way, trudging through the emptiness, trying to escape our problems with a few hits of cocaine?

My mother came to live with us, but life did not get any better. She had her own set of struggles, working on getting her life together. One night, after drinking and being up all night on cocaine, Luke and I got into a huge fight. He began storming in and out of the house, slamming things around. My mother grew concerned and called the police. Several cops showed up and attempted to remove the children from the house.

"No! What are you doing?" I cried frantically.

I raced toward the cops, and they jumped on me, pinning me down in front of my girls. The girls began screaming and crying as I struggled to free myself from the cops' grip. "Stop it!" I screamed. "Let go of me!"

But they did not let go. Instead, they dragged me outside, wrangling me like a calf. They slammed me down on the driveway, and I yelped in pain. They then tossed me in the back of the cop car and hauled me off to jail. I grew hysterical.

"You can't do this!" I screamed. "You can't do this to me!"

Once at the jail, the cops gave me a sedative to calm me down. They released me that night, and I walked down the street in my nightgown, still in a daze. Luke and the kids came to pick me up, and we continued fighting.

"How am I the bad guy here? You were the one who started all this! Those cops manhandled me like I was an animal!" I screamed.

The next night, angry with Luke and wanting to clear my head, I decided to go for a drive in his truck. I headed down the street, a thousand thoughts thudding through my head. *What just happened? This is all so crazy. What am I even doing anymore?*

I pulled over and wandered into a bar, where I began talking with a couple guys. They bought me a drink. Next, everything went black.

I woke up in a bed, rubbing my eyes groggily. *Where am I, and what just happened?* I glanced around the room, realizing I was in some sort of hotel. Then, looking down, I gasped in horror. I was naked and covered in my own blood. *What on earth is going on?*

I picked up the phone and dialed the operator downstairs. "I need help," I stammered.

I began frantically searching for my clothes. Noticing a name tag on the dresser next to the bed, I grabbed it for evidence. I then stumbled downstairs to the front desk.

"I need you to get me help," I begged. "Something bad happened to me."

The front desk clerk stared at me like I was from outer space. Angry, I grabbed the phone and dialed 911 myself. The police showed up, as well as an ambulance.

I relayed what little I knew about the two guys I'd met. The paramedics took me to the hospital, where they used a rape kit to collect DNA evidence.

The cops used the hotel's security cameras to track down the two perpetrators. Slowly, I pieced the horrific events of the night together. *Those guys drugged me and raped me. I can't believe it. This is a nightmare.*

"None of this would have happened if you'd just come home!" Luke cried angrily when I arrived home.

My father came and took our girls back to his house. The next day, CPS arrived, along with two police officers. They removed our son as well. We had officially reached rock bottom. Our kids were now gone, we had no money and life as we knew it would never be the same. The drug lifestyle had finally caught up to us, twisting us into its sick, dark web. *Where could we possibly go from here?*

☙☙☙

Luke

You have a choice, son.

I distinctly heard the words in my head, and I felt certain I knew where they came from. God was talking to me. I had not spoken to him much lately, but I still believed in him, and I knew exactly what we needed to do. I turned to Amanda, the smallest glimmer of hope entering me for the first time in a very long while. It was as if a light bulb had come on, shining brightly into a dark room, illuminating everything we could not see before.

"I know what we have to do," I said. "We need to give our lives to Christ. We need to start going to church and turning things around."

Amanda stared at me. "You're right," she said without blinking. "That's what we need to do."

We dropped to our knees and prayed right then and there, asking God to come into our lives. I had prayed the prayer years before, but I'd slipped back into a lifestyle of drugs and alcohol, putting God aside and living for myself. But after a long road of bad decisions, I realized that life had gotten us nowhere. Amanda and I both loved our children with every fiber of our being, but they were gone. We were broken and miserable, without a dime to our names. We had come to the end of ourselves, and we both believed Jesus Christ was the only one who could pull us out of our mess. Though Amanda had had very little exposure to God throughout her life, she prayed along with me, asking God for help.

"We need you, God. You are all we have. We're at the end of our rope. We're sorry for trying to do things our way. Help us to turn our lives around. We need you to save us."

And just like that, I believed he would. There were no magical fireworks shooting through the sky, but I knew something powerful had just happened. We had tried everything under the sun, when the very thing we'd needed — a relationship with Jesus — was the only thing we'd needed all along. He was the answer, and suddenly, we could see clearly. Without him, we were two messes, living selfishly, trying to fix things on our own. But on our own, we continued failing miserably, falling back into the same old patterns, hurting each other and those around us all over again. I saw how God, in his love, had sustained us through those hard times, protecting us when we put ourselves in danger. But we had still failed to seek him. That day, everything changed. We knew we could not live another second without him. Plain and simple, he was the answer.

I took Amanda to GTaustin, and it felt great to be back. The pastor and church members welcomed us the minute we walked in.

"Everyone is so nice," Amanda commented. "I'm in shock at how kind they are."

I smiled, remembering the many days I'd spent at the church in my youth. Though many things had changed since that time, much was still the same. The people were still kind, the message was still great and the church still had a huge heart for the community of Austin. *I wish I'd come back sooner. These people are like family, just waiting to bring us in. They really do care about us.*

A month after Amanda and I invited Jesus into our lives, she stood before the congregation and professed her new faith in God. Our pastor dunked her under the water, baptizing her as a symbol of washing away the old and ushering in the new.

"I was so nervous, but it was a wonderful feeling," Amanda gushed afterward.

From the moment we invited Jesus into our lives, we did not touch another drink or do another drug. I believe Jesus completely removed every craving we had, replacing it with an excitement for life and for him. We began working with the courts to regain custody of our children, doing everything we possibly could to become a family again. The state required us to take counseling classes and parenting courses and to comply with weekly drug testing. We complied with each thing they asked us to do.

Then I received a phone call that rocked my world. My beloved sister Chrissy had been killed in a head-on car accident while driving to Corpus Christi. At just 25, her life had been snuffed out. I called my parents, who were vacationing in Ireland, to deliver the terrible news. They flew back that night, and I picked them up from the airport. None of us knew what to do or say. The tears came freely, as we realized Chrissy would never be coming home again.

Our church rallied around us, offering prayers and kind words. I remained grateful for them, wondering how I'd ever gotten by without the support of a church family. Though the news of my sister's death devastated me, I clung to Jesus, knowing my hope was in him.

Ten days after Chrissy's death, Amanda and I went back to court. The judge, who'd worked our case from the start, delivered some good news. "I have never seen a case like yours in all my years of doing this," she said. "I grant you full custody of your children. This case is closed." She banged her gavel on the podium to finalize the decision.

Amanda and I stared at each other, tears in our eyes. We'd originally been told it might take two years to get our children back. This looked like a true miracle from God!

The judge waived the 30-day waiting period following the signing of Amanda's divorce papers, making it possible for us to marry right away. We ran out to get our marriage license and then called our pastor to see if he could perform a ceremony immediately. He agreed.

We married in a beautiful ceremony in a building on the GTaustin campus. Our friends from our new small group Bible study at church attended, as well as several other special people in our lives. I wished Chrissy could have been there to see me as a changed man. *She'd be so proud of me,* I thought with tears in my eyes as I glanced across at my beautiful bride.

I'm not the same man I once was. I'm a follower of Christ now, and I can't wait to start my new life with Amanda. The future awaits us, and this time, it's bright and full of hope. We can only go up from here.

ꙮꙮꙮ

Go up on that stage, Luke. Don't be disobedient.
I sat in my seat, shaking. *Okay, God, I'm going to do*

it. I am going to obey you and share what you've put on my heart.

I walked over to our pastor, who sat at the front of the church. "I think God wants me to speak a word of encouragement to the congregation," I whispered.

"Go for it!" he encouraged me.

I walked to the front of the room, still nervous as I cleared my throat. "I just feel like God wants me to share something with you this morning," I said. The minute I began talking, I felt a complete peace, and my nerves calmed. "Psalm 103 reads, 'Praise the Lord, my soul, and forget not his benefits — who forgives all your sins and heals your diseases and redeems your life from the pit.' My life was in the pit not long ago, but God redeemed it, and thanks to him, I have hope again. He can make everything new, no matter how bad it seems."

As I walked off the stage, I thanked God for giving me the courage to share with the church. When I'd left Teen Challenge, I'd been so excited about God, I felt sure I could go out and start telling others about him. But I'd slipped into my old habits, and that enthusiasm had waned. This time, I felt confident it was here to stay. *Maybe someday I'll get a chance to tell even more people about you, God,* I prayed. *Now that would be really cool!*

Life started to look very different than it did a short time before. Our marriage thrived, and Amanda and I intentionally sought out positive activities to do with our beautiful children.

We made a point to spend time outdoors, play in the

nearby creeks and rivers and watch movies as a family. We tried to eat dinners together every night, too, recounting our days and thanking God for his blessings.

Amanda's mom moved closer to us a few years ago, and their relationship has become so much better. They enjoy a true friendship now. Her mom doesn't gamble anymore, and she's an everyday presence in our lives, with phone calls and visits and being a good grandma to our kids. She's even come to church a few times.

I found good, stable work that I enjoy, which showed me again how God provided so faithfully for us.

We love GTaustin, where everyone, it seems, is excited about God. We put on a fall festival at our home and invited the neighborhood to join us for a barbecue. It was a great way to share the message of Jesus with them. We love our small group as well, where we share our struggles, pray for one another and receive encouragement. Our pastor encourages us to read our Bibles every day, knowing we will be strengthened by God's word.

As Amanda and I look back on our lives, we hardly recognize the people we once were. Amanda, forced to grow up too soon, spent years resenting her mother and father and trying to numb the pain with drugs, alcohol and men. She felt homesick for something, yet she never knew what that something was. Though I grew up knowing about God and sought him at different times in my life, I tried doing things my own way, seeking comfort in cocaine and other substances. In the end, we both wound up broken, penniless and depressed.

We found Jesus at the very bottom. He was our lifeline, and we clung tightly to him as he pulled us out of that pit and set us on our feet again. I learned it is never too late to find him. No matter how old we might be, no matter what horrible things we might have done, it does not matter. Jesus is always ready and waiting with open arms. And I'm so glad I fell into those loving arms.

A SONG FOR EMMA ROSE
The Story of Chava
Written by Rosemarie Fitzsimmons

I stood at the doorway to the exam room, staring at the metal gurney with its ominous-looking silver stirrups. Behind me, Dad and the doctor exchanged words in muffled tones. The two men came to some agreement, and then Dad pulled a roll of bills from his pocket, tossed it onto the doctor's desk and left the room without giving me a glance.

At the nurse's instruction, I entered the exam room, exchanged my clothes for a hospital gown and settled onto the cold gurney. Standing on my left, she covered my eyes with a brown paper towel just as the doctor stepped up to my right side. Before I could wonder why she'd done that, I received a quick shot in each arm.

Someone strapped my ankles to the stirrups and my wrists to the side railings. I didn't ask why. I didn't fully realize what was about to happen. I didn't understand any of it. I thought we'd come here for another prenatal exam.

"Don't moan, cry or scream ... or you may die." The doctor spoke to my paper towel-covered eyes, and I peered at him from underneath its bottom edge. He pulled a long silver instrument from a nearby tray.

"If you make any fuss at all, this could puncture the wall of your uterus. You will start hemorrhaging, bleeding, and if that happens — well, do you see that side door over there?"

"Yes."

"My nurse and I will go out that door, and you will probably bleed to death before anyone discovers you here. We will not call an ambulance or rush you to the hospital."

He took a seat at my feet, adding, "This will feel like severe pinching, like really bad menstrual cramps."

I gasped at the pain, both from the needle and from my father's betrayal. *Why did he trick me into coming here? Why hadn't he explained what was going to happen? Isn't this illegal? Why didn't they ask me one more time if this was my choice? Is Mom still in the waiting room? Does she know what's happening to me in here?*

After lying for what seemed like hours on that cold steel gurney, the torment ended and the doctor turned away. I watched his gloved hands scrub the silver instrument in a deep white porcelain sink.

I spoke to his white coat. "Do you know what it was?"

"What?" He glanced over his shoulder.

"A boy or a girl?"

"Oh." He turned back to his scrubbing.

"You haven't aborted the baby yet. That will happen naturally, sometime next week."

That procedure, and a similar one that followed one week later because the doctor was wrong, were probably the reasons I was never again able to have a baby.

ॐॐॐ

Neither of my parents knew how to love a child. They simply hadn't been taught. As such, I grew up an only child, desperate to know real love.

I was born in 1952, at Bergstrom Air Force Base in Travis County, Texas.

My mom delivered me alone because my dad, a military officer, was away on assignment.

Dad had been raised in the Masonic Home and School of Texas, in Fort Worth, from the time he was 6 years old, but he wasn't an orphan. When his own father died, neither his mother nor his grandmother was able to manage the care of six children. Grandma kept the baby, the oldest two tried to survive as best each could on his own and Dad and two siblings went to the Fort Worth home. He spent his childhood and adolescent years (during the American Depression) in institutionalized care and harbored a lifelong hatred toward his mother.

I never felt loved by my dad, but I loved him with a longing that began at age 3, when I learned what a daddy was and that I had one, but that he didn't live with me. I grew up wondering why my father had left and whether he loved me. Eventually, I decided he didn't love me or even like me. Or miss me.

My mom, too, was a product of the Great Depression and had known serious hunger. She told stories of eating only beans for supper and, some days, just the water the beans had been cooked in. In her eyes, I could commit no greater sin than to waste food. Despite the joy of being with my grandma and grandpa and other family members, I dreaded holiday dinners.

My mom would pile my plate with food from the extensive buffet, 10 times more than I could eat in a day. Those meals always ended the same way. Long after the rest of the family had cleared dinner away and settled in for card games, dominoes and football, I'd still be at the kids' table, sobbing and attempting to force food down while she cursed at me until every morsel was gone.

"You ungrateful bitch!" she'd growl. "Don't you *dare* waste one bite of this food!"

Family members, although clearly uncomfortable with her treatment of me, seemed afraid to confront her. They looked the other way.

Mom battled depression throughout her life, which manifested itself in mood swings and hoarding tendencies. I never knew what to expect with her. She would have manic highs and severely depressed lows, often oscillating between gaiety and a raging anger that could become violently abusive in a matter of seconds. When I was about 20, I learned from my mother's psychiatrist that my mom likely suffered from longstanding clinical depression, paranoia, possible schizophrenia, hypochondria and obsessive-compulsive behaviors.

I rarely saw my father. I was 18 months old when they divorced. I'd lived with my mother, while Dad, who married another woman several months after the divorce, went off to live and work in Hawaii. Even when he returned to Texas a few years later, I rarely saw him. As I grew up, I hoped against hope that he would want to see me and that he would come rescue me from life with my mother, but he did not. As it turned out, Dad's emotional behavior toward me was as unpredictable as Mom's. Our visits usually ended horribly, with him saying something mean. He just had no idea how to love. I latched onto a string of pretend daddies I saw on television: Danny Thomas from *Make Room for Daddy*; Jimmy Stewart from *It's a Wonderful Life*; Gregory Peck in *To Kill a Mockingbird*; and Brian Keith from *Family Affair*. In my pretend world, Daddy always had a hug for me.

Mom, on the other hand, loved me fiercely, in her own damaged way. I do have some sweet memories of my early years, such as sitting alone in a tiny pine rocking chair and singing hymns I learned in Mom's choir practices, being rocked gently in Mommy's arms while she sang to me and the two of us jitterbugging with broom handles or doorknobs and dancing as we sang a duet of "Me and My Shadow." However, I mostly remember the ways she hurt me.

I remember, at 3 years old, standing in our front yard in my seersucker pedal pushers and sleeveless top, holding a peeled banana. Mommy waved a white dishcloth at me from the dining room window.

"Hi, Mommy!" I waved as hard as I could, causing the top half of my banana to break off and fall to the ground.

I saw her face contort into rage. She rushed outside and stormed toward me, cursing loudly. "How dare you waste my food, you stupid, stupid girl!" She gripped my arm and dragged me through the screen door and into the dining room, where Dolly the maid was dusting our mahogany dining table. Mom shoved my face down, bent me over the seat of a matching mahogany chair and yelled, "Stay put!" while she raced to get a leather belt. Then she whipped my bottom, the backs of my legs, my arms and my waist, all while swearing and calling me horrible names that I didn't understand and screaming about her hard-earned money, how I had wasted precious food and how stupid I was.

That was the first time (as far as I remember), but similar treatment continued through my teenage years, almost daily. Even when I was a little girl, she'd curse at me, call me bad names, violently shake me and sometimes throw me — against a wall or our upright piano and, once, at the plate-glass window of a downtown department store. She'd grip my upper arms, digging her fingernails into my flesh until five bloody fingernail imprints stained each arm.

My body told the story, but no one ever read it.

Throughout my childhood, my face, neck and arms were covered in bright red, blistery welts; long, rectangular strap marks; baseball- and softball-sized bruises that would turn from blackish-blue and green to greenish-yellow and then fade to a grayed yellowish stain; puncture wounds from her sharply trimmed fingernails; and slap marks — entire handprints — on my face and arms. My neck has hurt throughout my life; this I believe came about because of my constant shaking. When I complained about it, my mother accused me of copying my dad, the way he used to rub his neck and hint for her to massage it. I always wondered if my teachers or other students ever saw the marks on my body. In those days, however, no one talked about child abuse.

I began praying and singing hymns to God when I was 3, especially after that first beating. I *so* wanted to believe God really existed and that he could rescue me. Even at 3 years old, I was a bruised reed by the water's edge blowing every which way in the wind.

෴

"Open the blue box first, Chava!"

I looked at the ordinary, bow-less package under the gaily decorated Douglas fir. It was the least intriguing to me, at age 7, yet Mom's excitement was infectious.

I sat on the cold linoleum floor right beside the cheap white angel hair blanket that my mom had draped around the base of the tree. Her Hallmark cardboard nativity manger with its chipped-paint ceramic nativity figures sat amid the gifts atop the angel hair.

Giggling with anticipation, I slowly lifted the lid. Out popped a tiny 10-week-old Chihuahua. I squealed with delight as the puppy wiggled and squirmed all over us.

"He's beautiful, Mommy! Just like a little fawn! Oh, thank you, thank you!"

Mom looked quite pleased with herself. "What do you think we should name him?"

I studied his wriggling, dancing form and decided immediately. "Prancer, after Santa's reindeer!"

The newly named puppy, excited to be released from his box and elated to meet his new family, danced over to the white angel hair blanket and relieved himself, quickly turning the pristine white to bright yellow.

Mom's eyes narrowed. My own eyes went wide with horror, knowing what might happen next. Cursing at him, she viciously snatched him off the floor, holding him with one hand at arm's length. She grabbed a newspaper, rolled it with the other hand and smacked him with it repeatedly. Then, her anger still not spent, she raced to her bedroom for her bristle hairbrush, striking him all over his fragile little body.

This was the first of many beatings during the tiny puppy's two years of life with us. Always, when the hysteria was over, my mom would bathe him in warm water in the kitchen sink and then wrap him in one of our terrycloth bath towels and sit in the mahogany rocking chair, rocking and singing baby lullabies to him, just as she'd do to me after a particularly horrendous beating.

Two short years later, during the early part of my fourth grade school year, I walked into the house after school to discover my mom wailing. She said she had come home from work to eat lunch and found Prancer had bled out all over the bathroom floor.

I screamed, "What do you mean, he bled out?"

She just kept repeating the phrase, adding while crying that she had rushed him to the vet, but the vet told her that both of Prancer's kidneys had ruptured. I cried inconsolably, as did my mom, for several days.

Despite Mom's outbursts, I loved her in my own way as best I could — and ironically, in a protective way. She provided me with shelter, nutritious food and nice clothing. She did not spend money on herself so as to provide me with myriad private and group lessons to develop the talents she saw in me. I will always be grateful for all she did that made my life's career possible.

As I grew older, I better understood about the demons she'd fought throughout her life. In addition to continual financial stress (while my father's business prospered), she mourned the loss of her promising youth. My mother had been a Blues singer, with a smoky alto voice, a "can-can" dancer for the Austin-area USO during the World War II era, an actress and an exquisitely beautiful woman. I have pictures of her wearing elegant evening gowns and long, formal gloves, dancing cheek-to-cheek with handsome men. During her rare playful times, I saw glimpses of her vibrant side.

After Mom divorced my dad, she sank into a reclusive hell. I can remember her crying and saying, "No one ever hugs me. No one ever touches me. No one loves me. All I'm good for is breathing air and taking up space."

When I was older, she'd grab the butcher knife and press it to her stomach and run through the house yelling that she wanted to die. I'd yell, too, for her not to kill herself. Eventually she'd lock herself, still screaming, in the bathroom, and I'd be on the other side of the door begging her to lay the knife down and come out of the bathroom. Then she'd come out, put the knife back in the kitchen drawer and stillness would descend upon the home — until the next time.

᠊ᡏᡏᡏ

The horn blared in our driveway, and I skipped out of the house, eager for my date with Walter. I couldn't wait to see what he had planned for my 17th birthday. For eight months he had been coming home every weekend from school and taking me out. I didn't particularly enjoy our dates, but I enjoyed having a boyfriend who was a senior at Texas A&M University.

"For Pete's sake, Chava, you know I hate to wait." His tone sounded particularly cold.

"Sorry. Where are we going?"

"The usual. Dinner. No movie, though."

Walter had been my first date — a blind date set up by an older friend. To this day, I don't know why Mom even allowed her 16-year-old daughter to go out with anyone nearly 21 years old, but I'd been thrilled to have someone show interest in me. I couldn't understand why the boys at school hadn't asked me out. After all, I was a pretty girl with a nice figure, I was bright and a good actor and dancer. Their rejection hurt. Dating Walter made me feel wanted.

Dinner was nothing special. A burger and fries. Walter talked very little, and we left as soon as we finished eating.

"Come on, I have something planned."

I smiled, and I opened the car door because he had already walked around to the driver's side. As I slid to the center of the front seat, he barely looked at me. We drove to the Catholic church, as usual, where he left me waiting 30 minutes. I once asked what he did there. His answer: "I go to confession."

I later understood how much he had to confess. Our previous dates had not been like the storybook scenes I'd expected. He often took me to a deserted place and forced me to perform acts that I didn't understand were wrong. At the time, I was scared and ignorant, and I thought this was what girlfriends did. He never crossed a certain line, though — I remained clothed.

On my birthday, we pulled into his parents' driveway, and I began to feel excited.

Oh, my, I'm finally going to meet his family. I pulled a brush from my purse and ran it quickly through my hair.

But the house was empty.

Walter took me to the master bedroom and made me undress.

"This might hurt," he said.

When it was over, I dressed, and he took me home. I never heard from him again.

I was much older when I understood that he'd been waiting for my birthday because it meant he wouldn't be charged with statutory rape.

Almost the next day, Rudy, the younger brother of a friend, swooped in and started to take me out. At first, I thought he was protective of me — he'd make me stay in the passenger seat of his green Mustang while he sold marijuana out of the trunk. Until I asked, I didn't know what he was doing, and when he told me, I still didn't really understand.

One fall afternoon, Rudy took me on a picnic in an open field. He brought a basket of fried chicken, and I set out one of my grandma's homemade patchwork quilts. We lay on the quilt for hours, talking about our dreams for the future. Despite all that happened a few weeks later, I counted that as one of my all-time sweetest dates.

In the second week of October, Rudy took me on a different sort of date, this time to a seedy downtown motel. He pulled his car right up to a drive-through window, reached out his arm and paid a man $3. We had not discussed this beforehand; however, still the naïve one, I followed as Rudy led me into a dark and dank room with a foul-smelling bed. The room was alive with fleas and cockroaches. For the next few hours, I lay there while he did what he'd probably planned all along.

Three weeks later, Mom cursed and beat it out of me: "Yes, I might be pregnant."

A local doctor confirmed not only that but a venereal disease, as well. That afternoon, my mom called my father and insisted that he needed to come and help her with me.

His answer was to find the doctor willing to perform an illegal abortion. This was before the Supreme Court decision that legalized the procedure.

When the initial attempt failed, I was taken back to the

same doctor, and he repeated the procedure. This time my father did not accompany me; he just left money and told my mom to handle it.

During the weeks that followed, I was in so much physical and emotional pain after destroying my baby that I sat in my room and cried. I cried for the baby, I cried because I felt dirty and worthless and I cried for the person I'd become.

One day, Mom had the Episcopal church women at the house to plan upcoming altar guild responsibilities. She came into my room and asked me not to cry because they would hear me. Then she sat down on my bed and started crying herself.

She told me that she, too, had an illegal abortion, before she'd married my father. As she recalled the details, she began to re-live the experience, and I realized that it was she who needed consoling. I held her and told her I was sorry for her, and I rocked her on the bed.

Much later, after my mother's death in 1990, my mom's sister asked why I thought I hadn't been raised in a Baptist church as they all had been growing up. Then I told her my theory.

"I think she believed she wasn't worthy."

ॐॐॐ

"Come on, you know this. What's the capital of Maine?"

Len sat on the carpet by the Christmas tree with his back against the wall, quizzing me from across the room so I couldn't cheat. Hair fell across one of his eyes with a dramatic flair. I thought, not for the first time, that he even *looked* like a theater major.

"Portlan — no, Augusta!" I couldn't help but laugh. It was so nice to have him there. I hadn't seen him much since he graduated high school.

"Good job, Chava. I think you've got 'em all. That's enough for tonight. You'll pass the test, I'm pretty sure."

Mom was still out on some errand or another. It had been only three weeks since the abortion. Len was being such a gentleman that I was able to relax. I appreciated the tutoring he'd given me over the prior week or so, but more importantly, I needed desperately to be with someone who was decent and who liked me as a friend.

We talked a bit, reminiscing about the time two years earlier when we'd acted together in our high school's performance of Steinbeck's *Of Mice and Men*. I'd been in 10th grade then, he a senior, and we'd become close friends during all the rehearsals. The conversation drifted to relationships.

"So, tell me, what kind of person do you see yourself marrying someday?" I wasn't trying to be coy; I was merely curious.

He absentmindedly brushed the unruly hair back into place.

"I don't know. Someone smart, funny, good-looking — someone who appreciates theater. What about you?"

"The same. Smart, funny, protective. Love of theater would be nice."

The room became quiet, and I hastened to fill the void. "Well, now, it sounds as if we're describing each other!"

Len raised one eyebrow. "Yep. So, do you want to get married?"

I laughed. "Well, okay, but maybe you'd better give me your high school ring first so people will think we're going steady."

He nodded and pulled the ring from his finger.

That was my so-called proposal.

In the weeks that followed, I passed my exam, and Len sold his trail bike to buy me an engagement ring. We had our first date two weeks later on New Year's Eve. A few months after that, we drove to Austin where he was to perform in a band. Later that night, he gave me the tiny diamond ring in St. David's Episcopal Church. He wanted to make it a solemn and religious occasion, he said.

We planned to wait at least a year before marrying.

One month and nine days later, and nine days after I graduated high school, I ran away from home, and our plans changed.

It happened during a church service. I had walked ahead of Mom on the sidewalk leading into the church. She flew into a rage, digging her fingernails into one of my arms and berating me in front of the congregation — using strings of profanity that included the Lord's name. Mortified, I left as soon as the service ended and ran to the parking lot. I drove to my father's house and never went back home.

I stayed with Dad for about two months — my first

time ever to "live" with him. Len was performing summer stock theater in Idaho. I called and told him what had happened and that I'd left home. He said, "Well, let's just go ahead and get married this summer."

And so we did.

꒰ꋊ꒱ꋊ꒱

The Sunday morning wedding ceremony was planned in less than a week and lasted 11 minutes. We had to finish before the church services.

I'd already started getting into my off-the-rack jerscy knit dress when Mom arrived, late as usual. Meredith, Dad's fourth wife, was helping me attach my veil. Mom yanked the veil out of her hand and began screaming and cursing, so Meredith walked out and went to sit with the guests. Still cursing, Mom snagged some poor soul standing nearby.

"Take a damned photograph of the mother of the bride putting on the damned veil!"

I still have that picture, in which a sad and mortified young bride cowers fearfully beside a woman with a forced smile and angry eyes.

My father walked me down the aisle. Eleven minutes later, as Len and I walked to the front of the church, he and Meredith slipped out the side door and left.

I don't know why Len married me. For my part, I was so damaged, I thought marrying some young man from a "nice" family was my ticket to a better life.

The lying started immediately. Once, when he was angry, he threw me face down on a bed and spanked me, humiliating me and calling me the same names my mother had called me since I was little.

We went to Idaho, where he had just won a scholarship. I took some courses at the University of Idaho, between my two part-time jobs. Len would often go to a pizza parlor/bar to pick up supper and stay inside for hours, while I sat outside in the cold car (I was underage). I tried to be a good wife, although it was hard to know what he expected of me.

We returned to Texas for the next semester at the University of Texas in Austin. I got a job as a file clerk earning a pittance. One day, I came down with the flu and called Len's school to ask him to pick me up, only to learn that he had dropped out months earlier. Every day, he'd been pretending to go to classes and attend rehearsals. At the end of that day, he picked me up at the usual quitting time. I got in the car and asked about his day, his classes, his rehearsals, and he regaled me with details.

Quietly, I let him know I'd called. He began cursing and flew into a rage I'll never forget. He banged his head against the steering wheel and began violently swerving the car back and forth — first into oncoming lanes, then back to the passenger-side curb. I was so afraid, I screamed and screamed and screamed.

"Len, stop! You're going to kill us!"

And then he *did* stop. He slammed on the brakes, coming to a screeching halt in the middle of a busy intersection, under a traffic light. Amid the din of squealing brakes and blaring horns, Len jumped out, leaving his driver's door wide open. He ran out in front of the car and started banging his fists on his head and yelling with his eyes shut tight.

I loved Len, despite the ill treatment, despite my suspicions that he was unfaithful (even while we were still in college), despite everything.

And despite everything, I came alive and blossomed. I attended six different colleges and universities over 13 years, but Len and I both finished college. I excelled in theater, speech and English and was hired to teach high school, even before I'd earned a teaching certificate. I later earned a master's degree and the required teaching credentials. I hadn't chosen teaching, but I wound up with a 28-year career in public schools, molding young minds and sparking their imaginations.

For the last nine years of our marriage, although Len would sometimes give me a quick kiss and would occasionally hug me or let me hold his hand, we did not engage in lovemaking anymore.

We lived practically separate lives. I was deeply wounded by this rejection. After 17 years of marriage, he divorced me and remarried three weeks later.

I lived alone for many years, believing I was just taking up space. I met a man through a dating service, but the experience turned out to be disastrous, as he was a con and a thief. He emptied all my bank accounts, joint accounts with my mother. My mother died during the ordeal. He went to jail, where he later died, but once again, I felt violated and rejected. It wasn't until I was much older that I had an encounter with Jesus that changed both my life and my direction.

સ્ર્સ્ર્સ્ર

Midnight. How could I possibly still be awake?

The bottle of Tylenol PM was empty.

Nothing on television held my interest.

I tried reading, which usually helped, and finished yet another cheap paperback before realizing, *I'm still awake.*

I was nearing retirement age, and I needed sleep if I was going to be able to focus in the classroom.

Instead, I folded my arms across my chest and gave in to my sour mood.

I'm just walking dead. I have no life. I have no purpose, other than to chase that piece of cheese called retirement. My life is just the same old dark nothing.

Quietly, suddenly and unexpectedly, I heard a male voice say, *Read the Bible.*

Only days later, upon reflection, did I come to understand that this had not been my own internal voice. Somehow, I felt compelled to obey. I reached for the palm-sized white leather Bible my mother had given me. I turned to the beginning, to the Book of Genesis.

Good idea. If this doesn't put me to sleep, what could?

Several times in my life, I'd set the lofty goal of trying to read the Bible. Each time, I would get only as far as the "begats" or the numbering of the tribes of Israel, and I'd put it down in frustration and boredom.

As always, I turned to Genesis, chapter one, verse one.

No, said the voice. *Begin with the New Testament, in the book of Matthew.*

All right, then.

I turned to Matthew, the first Gospel. The perfectionist in me grumbled and begrudgingly began in the middle of a book — in the Bible's case, where the New Testament started.

To my surprise, I understood it. I even found the storyline interesting. I must have fallen asleep eventually, but the next day, I could hardly keep my mind on the lessons.

Breaking a pattern of many years, I left school as soon as the bell sounded. I raced home and climbed into bed, still in the light of day, and picked up reading the Bible where I'd left off the night before.

Four days later, I was in the Book of Luke, reading a crucifixion scene yet again, for the third Bible book in a row. For a moment, I was disappointed.

Are these writers just going to keep repeating the same story?

Sure, there were some differences, I noticed. Luke did not go into the details of Jesus' hands and feet being nailed to the cross. In fact, when I came to chapter 23, I saw his only mention of nails, in verse 38: "A signboard was nailed to the cross above him with these words: This is the King of the Jews."

As my eyes landed on the word "nailed," I heard a loud rumbling sound like rushing wind, and a scene flashed and unfolded before me.

I was still in my antique king-sized bed in my bedroom, yet, simultaneously and inexplicably, I saw Jesus hanging on the cross, looking right at me — through time and space. Looking at me, in my white cotton nightgown in my bed.

I could only meet his gaze for a moment. I shut my eyes tightly as gut-wrenching tears rose from the depths of my soul, and I cried out to this man I'd only just met, "I know you, my brother, my friend!"

When I opened my eyes, the scene continued, and I watched Roman soldiers lower the cross back to the ground. They drove and pounded the long iron stakes through the flesh, muscle, bones, tendons and nerves of his two hands and his two crossed feet.

I felt the weight of each drive of each nail. Blood spilled onto the earth. I cried, "It's killing me to watch them doing this to you! I'm so sorry. I'm so sorry for your pain!"

The soldiers hoisted the wooden cross upright, and again, he looked at me. I knew he knew me, too, and I saw compassion and forgiveness in his eyes.

I cannot explain, to this day, what happened next. Somehow, I felt as if I were being "transported" to him. I collapsed, weak-kneed, into the dirt, alongside three other people. I was between two women. Shoulder-to-shoulder, I cried and grieved with them — they in their Biblical garb of the times, and I in my cheap white cotton nightgown from Walmart. I lifted my chin to gaze at Christ, who died for me, on his cross at Calvary.

I felt so sorry for everything I'd done that put him there.

"Will you forgive me? Will you please forgive me of all my sins? For stealing food and clothes and cosmetics? For lying to my mother and my husband? For dishonoring my father and mother?" On and on, I listed my sins — lust, gossiping, bitterness, unforgiveness — then I thought of my unborn child, whose sex I'd never learned. "For the abortion, Lord? I am so sorry that I've hurt you! I am so sorry. Please, please, forgive me!"

Crying, I scooped up some dirt I saw before me into the palms of both hands and lifted it to my face. I wanted to smell this dirt to see if it was real. I covered my face with my hands, and the dirt smeared and mixed with my tears.

Instantly, I found myself back in my bed.

On Palm Sunday, a few days later, I walked into the church called GTaustin. People of all ages and all walks of life were raising their arms, and they were kneeling and lying face down on the floor of the sanctuary.

Wow, these people look as if they really know there is a God! They look as if they are really worshiping him!

I tentatively raised my hands, too, as I sought to show my own love to Jesus.

In the weeks following, I joined a small home fellowship group where I asked questions incessantly, particularly about baptism, and I continued going to church.

During a church service at the end of May, the pastor had some of the church leaders line up in front of the altar and invited us to come forward to receive the baptism of the Holy Spirit. I didn't quite understand what he was offering, but with trepidation in my heart, I nervously walked to the altar area with a few other brave souls.

I stood before a lady in the line, who took my hands in hers and asked, "Why are you here?" I answered that I wanted to know who the Holy Spirit is. She rather sternly, at least to my sensitivities, explained that this was not a class but a baptism of the Holy Spirit.

I tried to pull my hands out of hers, but she held on. "I can still pray for you."

"No, thanks, I'd rather not."

I felt rebuked, embarrassed and stupid.

She prayed over me, but I refused to listen to her words. As she finished, she added that if I wanted to call the church and make an appointment to meet with her in her office, she would be glad to answer my questions.

I yanked my hands from hers and fled to my seat in the rear of the sanctuary.

Despite the tears of frustration welling inside me, I was determined to stay for the service, if only to counter my instinct to run away after feeling shame and rejection.

A woman sat next to me and began fanning my face. I realized that she must have seen me return to my seat and realized I was upset.

As I peeked at what this kind woman was doing to and for me, I suddenly became aware that the entire sanctuary was blanketed in a smoky darkness. I perceived no light at all, which frightened me. Then I heard a familiar voice, the one I believe to be God, say to me, *Stay seated. Your friend sits with you. Stay seated. Your friend sits with you.*

Just as I was about to bolt from the sanctuary, the pastor made an announcement, taking off his watch and tossing it across to his chair on the platform with perfect aim.

"Leaders, let's not rush. If anyone has questions, give him or her time to ask them. We don't want to rush the Holy Spirit."

This grieved me even more. *Why couldn't he have said that when I was up there, God? Why did I have to be the one cut out of this?*

So I bolted. A man tried to stop me in the parking lot, but I wouldn't return. I think that in my fragile state, I overreacted, and the people were all genuinely concerned about me.

I drove home and immediately took a nap. The stress had been overwhelming. When I awoke, I got out of bed and was walking toward the foot of the bed. Without warning or preconceived notion or any intention, my body twirled around to face a corner of the bedroom, and my voice, with a strength thus far unknown to me, shouted, "No, Satan! You will NOT keep me from being baptized!"

That statement, emanating from my own mouth,

surprised and shocked me. I had had no such thought in my own mind! I didn't talk to Satan — never had. If my entire life I had never even been sure whether or not God really existed, I sure as heck didn't believe in a Satan, much less speak to him.

I sank to my knees, folded my hands and said, "Jesus, I believe you. I give my life to you. I know who you are now. Thank you for revealing yourself to me in this bedroom. Thank you for coming to me when I hadn't even asked you to come. Thank you for coming to me when I didn't even know that you were the one I needed! I am yours, Jesus."

With those words, a new power came into me. I walked outside and, as I've since heard other new believers tell me, the greens were greener, the blues were bluer and every person I saw that afternoon was indescribably beautiful! I felt like Jesus was seeing through my eyes, and I through his.

How? I learned in reading my Bible that he had chosen me first, by name, long before I was even born. But I had chosen him back by receiving him into my heart and mind to dwell inside me as my personal Savior and my Lord.

I was baptized two months later.

At a spiritual retreat sometime afterward, I talked about my abusive upbringing, and I told the story of Prancer. Although I'd never stated it, even to myself, I'd grown up wondering whether my mother had killed Prancer during one of her rants. One of the ladies who listened to my story contacted me later and said she'd been praying for me and that she'd had what she called a revelation about Prancer's purpose in my life.

"Perhaps," she said gently, "he was there to take some blows meant for you. And perhaps, if your mother hadn't seen firsthand how deadly her abuse could become, she wouldn't have been able to rein in her anger when she was beating you. Prancer's death most likely served as a constant reminder to her, and he probably saved your life."

I believe she was right, as firmly as I believe God sent Prancer into our home for that purpose and also to be my only childhood friend.

ॐॐॐ

One day, I walked into Austin LifeCare, which offers services and counseling regarding pregnancy, parenting and post-abortion issues. It had been nearly six years since I'd accepted Christ, and I'd learned a lot about the Lord and received love and prayers and healing from others during those years. Now, I figured, it was my turn to help others. I told the woman who greeted me that I wanted to volunteer with her organization. She took my information, and when she learned that I'd had an abortion, she enrolled me in a 10-week post-abortion care Bible study.

The course was interesting and helped me address issues I'd not considered for many years. One chapter of homework near the end of the study suggested I write a letter to God about my abortion experience and tell him anything I wanted to say to my aborted baby. Another part of the assignment had us pray and ask God to reveal something about the child and to restore dignity to the child by giving him or her a name.

I prayed what I wanted most to know. The same question I'd asked the doctor many decades earlier when I'd been lying on that cold table.

Was it a boy or a girl, God?

Around 3 a.m., I woke up, startled. Something seemed to be there, whispering. As I became consciously awake, that familiar voice spoke in my mind, and I heard in a still, small, quiet way, *Your baby is a girl.*

I wept quietly, my heart filled with thanksgiving. I had a daughter.

I believed I would see her one day, and I agreed with the homework assignment — she needed a name.

A few days later, at an Easter dinner in the home of one of my best girlfriends, I was admiring her newly planted herb seedlings, one of which was rosemary. I told Kari about my upcoming assignment for the next Bible study meeting, which would be two days later.

As I inhaled the rosemary's deep, robust aroma, I said, "I've always liked the name Rose."

Kari responded in the quietest voice of her own, "Emma is a nice name."

"Yes, it is," I answered just as softly. I felt the breeze blowing through the trees, as if the wind was singing a lullaby through the leaves, and I knew. Emma Rose. That's her name. That's my baby's name.

৵৵৵

I came to Glad Tidings of Austin after meeting Jesus in my bedroom. Since then, I have come to think of GTaustin as my mothering and fathering church. The people there have consistently shown me love and helped me grow in the Lord, through discipleship, mentoring and encouragement. I went from having few friends to being part of a loving community with hundreds of friends. Now I think of my friends at GTaustin as my family.

I learned to see myself as God's chosen and cherished daughter. Never again would my body, mind or spirit be beaten and bruised, but the Lord himself would lay his hands on me and heal me. Never again would I be abandoned and rejected or cast aside as worthless and unloved. I no longer stood as a bruised reed at the water's edge, but as a strengthened reed in the hands of a loving creator.

He calls me "The Lovely One, Delightful One, The One Who Hopes." And I am, and I do! For I believe he loves me so, just as I believe he loves my little Emma Rose, and that one day we will sing together: "Jesus loves me, this I know, for the Bible tells me so!"

OVERFLOW
The Story of Jane
Written by Arlene Showalter

Home at last. I slipped my key into the front door, let myself into our apartment and flipped on the lights. "Are you home, Henri?"

Silence echoed. "Henri?" I wandered into the kitchen and then our bedroom.

"What is this?" I noticed the few wedding photos I'd set up in the apartment all lay face down. "This is weird."

I pulled out my cell phone and punched in Henri's phone number. "Where are you?"

"Hey, there, I'm at Allen's Pub. Come on down."

"I've been driving 11 hours. I'm really tired."

"Come on, it'll be fun."

May as well go down. I need some answers, anyway.

I slid in the booth across from my husband. A microsecond later, a young woman draped herself over Henri's shoulders. I waited for his outrage. Instead, he embraced her warmly and slid a hand inside her coat while murmuring something in her ear. I blinked several times to assure myself that I truly saw what I saw. I crossed my arms and waited for an explanation. None came.

I'm out of here. I rose and stomped to the door.

જ્જૈજ્

Dad was cruel and rough with Mom from my earliest memory. She, in turn, poured out her frustrations into my young ears — again, as far back as I can remember.

"Jane, you have to concentrate on your studies," Dad lectured as I ate my breakfast. "You'll never make it to the best universities unless you do."

"William, she's only in the second grade."

"What do you know? You're just a simpleton. You have no idea what higher education requires." Dad set his mug down with a resounding thud. "You wouldn't even have anything if I hadn't rescued you from that peasant village, so don't interfere."

જ્જૈજ્

I thought everybody's daddy berated the mommies and slapped them around, until I met Tina in fourth grade. She took me to her house where she flitted around like an un-caged bird. Nobody lectured her to be serious. *Her mom and dad even act like they like each other.* For the first time, I realized how normal families lived.

"Check this out," Tina said, applying lipstick and then puckering her lips.

"But I've never worn makeup."

"Then it's time you tried it."

We parked in front of the bathroom mirror and smeared eye shadow across our lids and painted blush across our cheeks. I turned my head side to side to inspect our handiwork.

"Okay, now it's time to hang out at the mall and check out the guys," I said jokingly.

I realized how abnormal my own home life was with my father filling one ear with lectures and Mom's constant complaints about him in the other.

At home, I remained silent and tense. Only at Tina's could I laugh out loud.

Tina and her older sister Leila lived easy-breezy and welcomed me into their warm circle. Leila drank, so we drank. Leila smoked, so we smoked. Tina taught me how to lift cigarettes free of charge from convenience store counters.

So, it was quite natural that when Leila started smoking pot, we joined her. I inhaled deeply, and for the first time in all my 13 years, I felt my body relax. The constant cacophony of Dad's instructional discourses and Mom's tearful what-am-I-doing-wrong and what-can-I-possibly-do-to-please-your-father laments vanished.

Wow. This is great stuff.

"Step it up, Jane," Dad snapped as I struggled in the hot Florida sun.

"It's so hot."

"Running this 5K will build your body *and* character, so buck up."

I snapped my mouth shut. I knew if I complained any more, Mom would receive the brunt of his wrath the same as the "whipping boys" of history. Besides, she had my 1-year-old baby sister, Irene, to tend to.

"Today is my first day of vacation," Mom announced on a Monday in the fall. She sighed deeply. "I need the rest."

"Can you drive me to school today?"

"Not today, Jane. I'm too tired." She sighed again. "Maybe tomorrow."

I dragged myself outside and mounted my bike. *I'm the only kid in the whole school who has to ride a bike to school. This sucks.*

A car struck me just as I approached the school's neighborhood. An ambulance rushed me to the hospital to address my injuries.

"Jane, Jane!" Mom raced to my bedside. "I'm so sorry. I heard about a bicycle/auto accident over the radio. I knew it was you and came as quickly as I could."

I touched the bandages on my face, wondering how much damage they hid. *May as well kiss boys goodbye. Nobody's going to want to date a girl with a damaged face.*

When I returned home to finish recuperating, Dad traded his lecturing tongue for gentle hands as he carefully dressed my wounded face every day.

"Finished," he said with a final, tender pat. Moments later, I heard his angry voice pierce the walls.

"You moron. Why didn't you buy more bandages today? We're almost out."

৵৵৵

"Come on, I'm taking you to Granny's," Dad said right after my face healed. I knew better than to ask why. Once we arrived, Dad sat me down in her living room.

"Your mother has moved out," he said, his hands shaking. "She's asking for a divorce. Your sister's going to stay with her and you with me until we figure the situation out."

Wow. I guess I wasn't important enough to take, too.

As bad as abandonment made me feel, the situation worsened when Dad began substitute teaching in my school. He was charming but strict, and other classmates begged me for the answer keys to his quizzes, to which I had *no* access.

Already beyond quiet, I felt further ostracized when my classmates began avoiding me because I was *his* daughter. We walked home from school together every day, stopping at a local convenience store where Dad purchased a six-pack of Coors beer and two packs of cigarettes. He drank and smoked and paced around the house, thinking aloud to process his thoughts — especially regarding their separation — while I labored over my homework at the dining room table.

৵৵৵

Eighth grade graduation arrived. My heart pumped with excitement as I lined up with the other graduates. My granny handed me a bouquet of flowers moments before we started our march into the auditorium.

"What's this?" I asked.

"It's from your mom. There's a card." She looked away.

Sorry I can't be there. Good luck. Mom.

"I'm sorry." Granny moved forward to hug me.

"Leave me alone." I stiffened and bit my bottom lip "Don't touch me." Tears rolled down my cheeks. *Buck up, Jane. Do you want people to see you crying?*

I lifted my chin and marched in with the other graduates. *Buck up.* I could hear Dad's voice in my head. *I know why Mom's not here. She's avoiding Dad.*

Only in the safety of my bedroom did I let my emotions loose. I jammed my recently healed face into my pillow and cried for hours.

"Your mother and I have resolved our differences, so you and I will move into the apartment she's renting," Dad told me. "We're moving in with Irene and her this weekend."

Mom's apartment had two bedrooms. Irene slept in one, and I in the other. Mom and Dad took the sleeper sofa in the living room. Quite inconvenient for a teen bent on looking for a good time outside the home.

It's 4 a.m. I hope I can pull this off.

I let myself in the front door when I was 15 after being out most of the night with friends from school. In the dim light of the streetlamp, I saw Dad sitting on the edge of the pull-out, arms crossed.

"We'll talk about this tomorrow. Go to your room."

Dad stretched his usual two-hour you-have-to-study-hard-to-get-a-scholarship-to-the-best-schools lecture into four.

"You're going to amount to nothing if you keep up with this foolish behavior. Don't you dare cry. You buck up and listen to me."

Mom tried to offer me a drink. Dad scowled. She put it down and retreated. Even the call of nature failed to move him from his resolve.

"You stay put until I'm finished talking."

Afterward, he said, "Now you are going to clean every book in my library, with a Q-tip, and put them all back — in alphabetical order."

๑๑๑

"We're sending you to France for your 10th grade," Dad informed me.

"Why?"

"I want you to have the international experience. It'll go far on your college applications. You'll stay with your mother's parents. It's perfect."

He doesn't care if I have to leave my friends behind. All that matters to him is education, education, education.

"It's time to come home," Dad announced after I'd completed my first year abroad.

"I don't want to. I like it here in France." *No need to tell him about my new boyfriend. That would send him into orbit.*

"You don't have a choice," Dad said. "I've decided to send you to Stony Brook in New York."

The same boarding school you went to? Are you kidding me? What did I do to deserve this punishment?

"Why?"

"It's college prep, and for sure you'll get a well-rounded and high-quality education. I've already made the necessary arrangements."

Thanks for taking my desires and feelings into consideration. Well, I guess the good news is that it'll put 1,100 miles between me and my dysfunctional parents. I think I just might like this decision, after all. Dad can't keep tabs on me like he does at home or even when I'm in France. Yes, this just might work.

I settled into Stony Brook, and in no time, the other partiers and I found creative ways to satisfy our thirst. We hid our six-packs of beer behind the gravestones in a nearby cemetery. I joined the acting club, knowing how Dad felt about it. *Total waste of time. I should be focusing on all the college apps I have to fill out and the coursework.* I shrugged and reveled in the newfound freedom of playing someone else.

"If my dad calls, tell him I'm in the library," I told my roomie as I scooted out of our dorm room to rehearse our school play.

"Not a problem. Break a leg!"

"So, you're William's daughter." The history teacher studied my name on his roll sheet.

"Yes, sir."

"You have some pretty big shoes to fill," he said. "I taught him when he studied here. The man's a genius. President of his class. Both Harvard *and* Duke offered him scholarships."

And now all the genius can do is make life totally miserable for his wife and two kids.

"We are all going to drive up to tour all the prospective colleges," Dad informed me the summer before my senior year. As we drove from campus to campus, Dad lectured me on the importance of education and character and success. Finally, I could endure the torture no longer.

"Put me on the train. I want to go back to Stony Brook. Right now."

"Class doesn't start for two weeks, and we have more colleges to visit."

"I'll go to Holyoke. So let me go back to Stony Brook right now because the dorms are already open." My heart pounded as I stood up to my dad for the first time. *I hope Mom doesn't pay for this, but I can't take any more.*

"Then, I'm going to choose Mount Holyoke. It's an all-girls college. That should help keep you focused."

I shrugged. "I like the campus. I'll go there."

❧❧❧

After completing my second year at Mount Holyoke, I signed up for a two-year study program in France. I wanted to return to my mother's home country to study the oral history of the daily life of women there.

I settled in with my grandparents again and breathed in the un-stifled French air. *Now, there's an ocean between us — again. Let freedom ring!*

My hands shook as I eagerly opened the latest letter from my fiancé, John. *Dear Jane,* he wrote, *I'm sorry to write this, but I'm a Christian now, and I met a woman who's also a Christian. I am deeply sorry that I was sexually active with you. I'm determined to do it right this time and will wait until Lucy and I marry to consummate our relationship. I wish you all the best. John.*

A friend from boarding school called a month later to tell me a good friend had died of a brain aneurism.

Right after that, my mom called to tell me my aunt had wrapped her car around an oak tree. She survived but needed a long convalescence.

Then, it was my turn to call Mom. Her father, whom I called Pepe, had died of lung cancer.

❧❧❧

Four emotional blows in as many months. Something snapped in me after Pepe's funeral.

I took the college money Mom had given me for my

studies and disappeared into Europe. I ran with gypsies. I crashed on the beach. I found a street artist and lived with him in his truck.

My money ran out in Slovenia, so I worked as a nanny until I saved enough to return to France.

"Where have you been?" Grandmother cried. "We've all been worried sick."

"I just had to get away to think." Her hysteria failed to move me when I showed up at her doorstep after a three-month absence.

"I don't want to come home," I told Dad in a phone call.

"You absolutely *will* come home," he retorted. "If you don't finish your bachelor's degree, it will be the most colossal mistake you've ever made."

"I like it here in France."

"I'm not going to sit by and watch you ruin your opportunities."

We argued — long distance — for more than three hours. Finally, Dad's voice softened. "Jane, I promise you, if you will come home and don't like it, I'll buy you a plane ticket to return to France."

I stepped into his trap and returned.

ɂɂɂ

"I miss you." Henri, my French musician boyfriend, called soon after my return.

"It's only three months until September," I said. "Then you can come, and we'll be married."

He flew over as planned. I smuggled him into my all-girl college dorm, and I taught him English between classes. I studied while Henri spent his days on the computer in our room and created music.

After the college learned of my French contraband, we found an apartment together. We decided to squeeze a wedding in during my final exams and hopped down to the courthouse.

"You need to marry us right now," I told the judge.

"Can't I at least go home and change first?" she asked with a smile.

"No time. I've got another final in three hours. We need to hustle."

෨෨෨

Henri and I moved back home to Florida after my graduation. No matter how hard I searched, no teaching jobs opened up, so I hosted at a restaurant and then landed a job at the post office call center to support us both until INS cleared Henri with a green card. Finally, he got a job in a theater, but we struggled financially.

There has to be something better than this, I thought as I surfed the Internet. *I remember how much fun it was to teach Henri English. Maybe I can find a job teaching other people English.*

I can do this, I thought as I browsed the University of

South Florida's Web site, which offered a degree in ESL (English as a Second Language). *It would be easy for me since I'm already fluent in French and English.*

Full-time coursework along with a part-time job at the university stressed me out until I remembered my old relaxing agent — pot.

Henri moved up to a job in programming, and we began partying away the extra money.

"What do you think of moving to Texas?" I asked Henri.

"What's in Texas?"

"I'd like to get a Ph.D. in linguistics. The University of Texas in Austin offers a program. Austin is a big dot com area and live music capital of the world, so there would be plenty for you, too."

He shrugged. "Yeah. Okay."

We settled into Texas life, taking our old patterns of school, work and party, party, party with us.

ॐॐॐ

"There's my exit. Ten more minutes and I'm home." I stretched my neck and shoulders with a sigh. *Eleven hours on the road is just too long a drive. I can't wait to relax and share a beer with Henri. Life is good. I'm getting my advanced degree. I love my cool musician husband, and we both have good jobs.*

I rounded the corner to our apartment and found

myself grinning even before I cut the engine. Even with travel fatigue, I quickly walked up to the porch and unlocked the door.

Why aren't the lights on?

"Henri, are you home?" I moved from room to room. *This is odd. He knows I'm coming in around this time. Where could he be?* I fished my cell phone out of my handbag and dialed his number.

"Henri, I'm home. Where are you?"

"Down at Allen's Pub. Come on down."

"I just got in. I'm beat."

"No, no. Come on down."

"Okay. I could use a drink."

Ted, the owner, and Jax, the bouncer, met me at the entrance. "Hey, guys," I said. I knew both well and saw them more as friends than business people.

"It's great to see you," Ted said.

"Thanks." *And why are you two meeting me outside?* Jax seemed to block the bar entrance.

My eyes narrowed. "What's going on, guys? You're acting weird. I'm going in to have a drink with Henri."

I pushed past both and stepped into the bar. After a few moments of scanning for my husband, I located him. I walked over and slipped into the seat across from him. Just as I ordered a drink, a young woman walked over and draped herself over Henri's shoulders.

"Excuse m ..." The words died on my lips when Henri wrapped his arms around her in a tight hug.

"If you want to save this marriage, meet me outside in

two minutes." I stood up and stormed out. Henri sauntered out, *five* minutes later.

"You sleeping with that girl?" I crossed my arms and leaned one hip against my car.

"No, no. You're crazy."

"We need to talk — right now." I opened the passenger door. "At home."

After persistent grilling, Henri admitted everything. I learned that Valerie was only the latest in a long string of conquests that started as soon as he arrived in America.

For the next month, I survived on cigarettes, Dr. Pepper, alcohol and pot, while I tried to sort out the shreds of my marriage.

I found out that Valerie waitressed in a local family restaurant that Henri frequented. I went and requested her booth. Valerie had no choice but to take my order.

"Do you love him?" I gazed straight into her eyes.

Her eyes flitted down.

"You thought he'd marry you? Did you know he's already married?" I balled both fists. "Do you realize what you've done to my marriage?" I demanded.

"I'm sorry. I'm sorry." Her eyes filled with tears. "I didn't know he was married. I swear."

"Don't you ever go near him again."

"Yes. No. I promise."

As I left the restaurant, revelation hit me. *No matter how many times I've told Henri that I love him, he's never initiated those words. Never. I'll give it 60 days to see if Henri really wants to save our relationship.*

I studied him with new eyes and observed no remorse in any of his behavior.

"This marriage is over. I'm leaving."

I chose Valentine's Day to move out.

While I anesthetized myself with whiskey, Henri moved on and found another girlfriend. I threw myself into one meaningless relationship after another.

ॐॐॐ

Two years later, my colleagues and I flew south to teach a summer program for the University of Texas in Mexico. We celebrated the graduation with plenty of Mexican booze and marijuana.

The next morning, I stumbled to the office of one of my co-workers. "Tom, I feel like crap."

"It's just a hangover. You got pretty wasted last night."

"I've been wasted plenty of times. This is different. I have massive pain here." I swept a hand over my abdomen. "I really need to go to the hospital and find out what's wrong with me."

"I'll get a cab."

Tom and some other colleagues accompanied me to the hospital. Through a translator, the receptionist demanded a credit card.

"I don't have one," I gasped, doubling over with pain. "I'm maxed out."

Without a word, another colleague handed over her own card.

"How can I ever repay you?" I asked between gasps.

"Don't worry about it. We just need some answers. Right now."

The doctors performed exploratory surgery and discovered I had a burst appendix and peritonitis — my abdomen had filled with blood.

"When did the pain begin?" the doctor asked later, again through a translator.

"I don't know. Maybe three or four days ago."

I didn't need a translator to read the look on his face and the one finger he held up. "One more day, and you'd be dead."

❧❧❧

The following year, the company I taught for held a retreat in the Texas Hill Country. Of course, the booze flowed faster than the Rio Grande. *Just call me Happy Hour Queen.* I snagged a glass of wine. And another. And another.

"Hey, Jane. Get up on that railing and perform a ballet routine," another partier dared me, three bottles of wine later.

"Sure will." I hopped up in a skinny minute and delivered several pirouettes. "You didn't think I could, did you?" I asked, grinning as I reached the end of the railing.

"Here, let me help you down." She reached up a hand.

"Nope. I can do it." At that moment, I jumped and landed hard on both heels on the wooden deck. "I'm okay," I insisted. "Let's party."

Three weeks later, I could no longer ignore the intense pain in both feet and went to a doctor.

"You broke both heels," he said, studying the X-rays. "When did you do this?"

"A week or so ago." *No way I'm going to let him know it's been three times that long. He'll judge me.*

"Well, you waited a week too long. You'll be grounded for a while."

I had to ice down my feet every day, experienced extreme pain each time and spent weeks in a wheelchair. Then, I graduated to a walker and finally a cane.

☙☙☙

"You up for a party?" Jim, a guy I barely knew, asked.

"Party? You know me. Happy Hour Queen. Count me in."

He scribbled an address on a scrap of paper. "I'll meet you there. Eight o'clock. Crystal's house."

"I remember her. We met at a party a while back."

"Right. We'll have a blast."

I should take a hostess gift with me. Hmmmm. I finally selected three bottles of wine. Two for me and one for Crystal.

Over the next six hours, I consumed more wine than I brought, along with countless rum and Cokes, numerous tequila shots and several joints.

My bladder complained, and I staggered to the bathroom, totally wasted. The moment I closed the door behind me, my body exploded. Blood, urine, vomit and feces sprayed the toilet, the walls, the floor and the sink.

After some clumsy, drunken efforts to clean myself and Crystal's powder room, I leaned against the door, searching for a strategy to extricate myself, unnoticed, from the party.

I think I can pull it off if I act nonchalant. With the guests congregating in the kitchen and on the patio, it could work. The front door is just steps away.

Two feet from my goal I heard a shriek.

Shit. Crystal must've seen her bathroom. I reached for the knob.

"What the hell are you doing?" Crystal rushed to block my escape, but backed up when she got a whiff of me. She flung open the door. "Get out of my house!"

"I need my keys," I mumbled.

She split and returned a few moments later. "Get the hell out of here, and never come back." She dropped the keys in my hand.

I stumbled outside and somehow bent my fingers back. Alcohol blocked any pain. I found my car and jammed the key in the ignition.

I awakened the next day, sprawled out on my living room floor.

What, what? I tried to sit up and clutched my aching head. *Ugh! What is that horrible smell?* Understanding penetrated my foggy mind as memories of the party and subsequent bathroom fiasco returned.

How did I ever get home? Why is my hand throbbing? What happened?

I crawled upstairs and into the shower. Afterward, I fell into bed — and awakened three days later.

I need to kick the drinking, I decided. *I can't keep hurting myself by getting wasted.*

My drinking friends disappeared from my life after I quit drinking. No bars. No parties. No buddies.

Now I returned to an empty house after work and cried my eyes out.

I'd better ice them down, I decided after catching sight of my swollen eyes in the bathroom mirror.

I started rocking my body through the violent weeping and touching things over and over again.

Maybe I'm autistic, I thought to myself. I began devouring articles on the subject.

Fits me to a tee, I concluded. I withdrew further.

❧❧❧

"How are you doing?" my friend Hannah asked later that same year.

"Don't even ask." I kept my gaze to the side of her. Eye contact with anyone unnerved me.

"Would you come to church with me?"

I shrugged. "Sure."

"Great, I'll call you on Saturday to confirm." Her light laughter sent a flicker of warmth through me.

"Okay."

"Sunday, then."

"I guess."

I threw out flimsy excuses three Sundays in a row. I awakened on the fourth with a deep sense of guilt. *I've promised Hannah repeatedly that I'd go to church with her and then make stupid excuses not to. She deserves better treatment than this.* I reached for my cell phone.

"I'll go to your church this morning."

"Good. It'll be great to see you again. I'll meet you there."

"Okay." I drove into the parking lot of GTaustin filled with dread. *What am I doing here? I don't want to go in and face a bunch of smiling people who all have their act together.*

Hannah saw me drive in and came over to my car.

"I'm glad you came," she said, smiling. "Let me show you around."

We toured the building and then she led me into the worship center. I sat between her and her sister-in-law. *I feel trapped. Why didn't I insist on sitting on the end?*

"If you don't understand something," Hannah whispered as the band assembled on the stage, "just ask me. I'll tell you anything you want to know."

The moment the music started, my tears cut loose. I felt like buckets of water cascaded down my face as the musicians sang a song that said we are worthy because Jesus makes us worthy.

Two days later, I remembered the lyrics of another song from that Sunday, "Let's worship and show him how we feel."

Yeah, right, God. I'll tell you how I feel. You abandoned me. You stuck me in this life with an overbearing father and a mother who continually burdened me with her unhappiness. You made me a loser. You let me marry a loser. My life sucks, and I'm tired. Tired of it all. Tired of working. Tired of crying. Tired of living. Tired of feeling totally abandoned and isolated. My life is a pile of shit just like what I let fly at Crystal's house. Thanks for nothing, God.

I staggered into the shower and turned the water on full blast. My arms felt like galvanized pipe, too heavy to lift above my waist. A sense of urgency pierced my befuddled mind.

Everyone tells me I need to surrender to Jesus, and he will somehow make everything clean and good and okay. Well, I'm a worthless mess, so if you want this pile of mess, God, you can have it.

I closed my eyes, too weary to stand alone any longer. I bent forward until I felt the wall, and leaned my whole weight into its solid presence. I breathed deep for some minutes, expecting nothing and *something* to happen. I felt no cleaner. I felt no hope. I felt *nothing*. With a sigh I opened my eyes. My body remained at an angle, leaning against — *nothing*. My whole weight stayed at that angle, resting against thin air.

"What?" I looked around and straightened up. "That's

impossible. I had to fall. I must fall." Understanding raced in, and tears joined the water cascading over my body.

"You held me, didn't you, Jesus? *You held me.*"

My hands trembled as the depression lifted. I lifted my arms over my head. "Thank you!" The overwhelming anger I felt against my parents washed down the drain. The numbing grief over my failed marriage followed. All the lies and signs of autism melted away as well. I shampooed my hair, washed my body and stepped out of the shower.

"I handed my life over to Christ," I told Hannah when I saw her at church the next Sunday. "I'm still not sure how I feel about that, but I know that I feel better and more stable somehow."

Week after week I attended GTaustin, and every time, I cried. I put all the emotional baggage on the table and asked God to take over.

People surrounded me and supported me with their arms and hearts. I felt their loving welcome starting with my first visit — from the woman who greeted me at the door like we had known each other for years to the small group leader who made sure I felt included.

❧❧❧

"Would you be willing to share your testimony with the church?" Pastor Kermit asked me some months later.

"Sure, if you think I can be of help." I tried to settle the nerves in my stomach. *This is the least I can do since Jesus did so much for me.*

Afterward, so many people came up to me explaining how much my story touched their own hearts.

"I loved your testimony. Thank you for sharing."

"Thank you for showing what Jesus can do."

"You allowed yourself to be transparent. You really moved me. Now I know Jesus can help me, too."

I smiled at the members of my new family. God's loving, accepting, appreciative family who treated me as a valued and beloved equal.

Yes, I decided, *I will sing from the overflow in my heart. I will sing that with joy and thankfulness. Let me tell you what Jesus did for me and what I know he can do for you.*

STRANGER IN MY OWN LAND
The Story of Halim
Written by Karen Koczwara

"You should be killed!" the guy screamed, tightening his grip around my neck. He yanked the collar of my jacket, his breath hot against my skin.

I tried to stay cool, but my heart raced. *I was not prepared for this. Where did this guy come from, anyway?*

"Let him go!" my cousin interjected. "Let's talk to him first, and maybe he will come back to Islam."

I won't. I never will.

"If we hear that you evangelize others, you will be killed!" the man threatened again.

Just then, I heard a knock on the door, and I breathed a sigh of relief. I wriggled out of the guy's grip and escaped. But as I headed down the stairs, adrenaline pumping through my veins, I knew this might not be my last such encounter.

Next time, I might really get myself killed.

They are watching my every move, waiting for me to slip up.

I am not safe anywhere.

అఅఅ

I was born in Morocco. My father's father was a descendant of the prophet Muhammad, a significant honor in our family line. My father worked hard as a farmer in France and was often gone for long periods of time. My mother stayed home to take care of my three sisters and me. When I was born, my mother's mother lived with us, as did her sister, husband and their children. The women all shared the household duties, including cooking, cleaning and washing our clothes by hand. Having several generations under one roof was not uncommon in our culture.

We lived in a large two-story house. The first floor included a courtyard area, washroom, kitchen and main living room, as well as two bedrooms. The upstairs was comprised of six bedrooms, as well as a rooftop area with another bedroom. We enjoyed family meals together and did most everything else together, too. We watched TV only to get our news but did not own any computers or electronics. My grandmother was the first one who introduced us to Quran recitation school.

I began playing soccer as well, playing on the soccer field a mile from my house. I also kicked the ball around the house, which did not make my parents happy. I loved having plenty of family around. My cousins became like built-in best friends, and my uncle stepped in as a father when my own father went away.

Like 99 percent of the Moroccan population, I grew up in a devout Muslim home. Each morning before my regular school classes, I went to the school of Quran, where I studied my religion. At 7 years old, I joined a school where we studied Arabic and the Quran. We also studied social studies and the geography of Morocco. By third grade, I began studying French as well. I also went to the mosque every single day to pray, as was tradition in our Muslim culture. I knew no other way and never dared question my religion.

When I was in middle school, my father returned from France and found work locally in the construction industry. I began high school and started studying English, along with my other subjects.

During my second year of high school, one of my friends who was doing correspondence with a Christian organization in Norway received a Bible translated into Arabic.

"You shouldn't read that," I told my friend. "You have the Quran." I asked him if I could have it. I intended to take it from him and hide it in the house, as I knew neither of us should be reading such a thing. But curiosity got the best of me, and I took a peek at a few of the pages. I read the story of Moses, a man who Muslims believe God used to reach many people in a powerful way. I put the Bible away and did not think much of it for a while, but the stories stuck in my mind.

My cousin went to France and came back with a New Testament Bible in French. I took it later from him surreptitiously and read most of it, which motivated me to return to the Arabic Bible that I received from my friend, and I began to read it daily, at least one chapter or two.

During my last year of high school, the teacher of my Islamic studies class began discussing the story of Moses. "The Bible says that God ordered Moses to kill children. This could not be the word of God."

I raised my hand. "But that is what God told Moses to do," I protested.

The teacher raised an eyebrow. "How do you know this?"

I gulped and sank down in my seat. *I can't tell her I read the Bible.* I did not say anything else.

After class, a girl approached me. "Did you read the Bible?" she asked.

I hesitated, unsure how much to divulge. "Yes, I have read it."

"Who gave you the Bible? Are you a Christian?" The girl continued firing questions at me. "Why do you Muslims pray to Muhammad?"

"Are you not a Muslim?" I asked, taken aback.

"No, I am a Christian," she replied with a smile. "My parents are Moroccans, but they converted from Islam to Christianity in the 1960s."

"Oh, wow." I didn't know what else to say. I did not know any other Christians. I was surrounded by Muslims everywhere I went. Meeting a Christian in my city was nearly unheard of.

That day, I went to one of my Islamic leaders, trying to better understand the study of the Quran. I began asking him many questions. He guided me to someone who was an expert in Comparative Religion. He had a Ph.D. in

Qur'anic studies and had studied the differences between Islam and other religions at great length. He also gave me several books about Christianity and taught me some techniques for how to debate with Christians. In my heart, I knew I belonged to the one true religion, but the conversation with that girl had spiked my interest in Christianity, and I wanted to make sure I knew how to defend my faith when it came down to it.

I began reading every piece of literature I could get my hands on. I also began watching videotapes of a man named Sheikh Ahmed Deedat.

A South African writer originally from India, Sheikh Deedat was a Muslim missionary who held numerous inter-religious public debates with evangelical Christians, most of which centered on Islam, Christianity and the Bible. He also established the IPCI, an international Islamic missionary organization, and wrote several booklets on Islam and Christianity.

In 1986, Sheikh Deedat debated popular televangelist Jimmy Swaggart in Swaggart's hometown of Baton Rouge, Louisiana. Nearly 8,000 people attended the event. He also debated well-known Christian preacher Josh McDowell and later challenged Pope John Paul II to a public debate in the Vatican Square. But the Pope did not take him up on the challenge.

I listened to the debates, soaking up every word. In my mind, I felt I knew the truth. *Islam is the one true religion. I'm just gathering information so I can defend myself.* The basic pillars of Islam had been ingrained in me since I was born. I believed that Islam was the complete and universal version of a primordial faith, revealed many times throughout the world, including through Adam, Noah, Abraham, Moses and Jesus, who we were taught were all prophets. We believed the Quran was the unaltered and final revelation of God. I was keen to practice all the pillars of Islam in the right way, except I didn't go to Mecca for the pilgrimage. I learned the basic concepts and obligatory acts of worship and strictly followed the Islamic law. I had never questioned my faith before, as I'd seen no reason to. I was a Moroccan Muslim, and that was as certain as the color of my hair and skin.

But something had shifted in my heart since meeting that girl in my class. I was intrigued by her and her Christian faith. She seemed like an anomaly, a one-in-a-million case. Could Christian and Moroccan really go hand in hand?

I continued talking with the girl, who introduced herself as Samia. She introduced me to her brother Ilyas.

"We grew up in a Christian home and never studied the Quran," he told me. "We only studied the Bible."

We began discussing Christianity and Islam at great length. We compared the differences in our religions. Ilyas talked about Jesus as God's son, a man who God had sent to earth to die for everyone's sins. Ilyas described his God as loving, merciful and forgiving. This was contrary to the message I'd heard about Christians growing up. Everyone, from my parents to my teachers to the Moroccan Muslim society, described Christians as lost people since they don't convert to Islam. *They do not have the truth,* they said. But Ilyas and his sister seemed so different. They seemed genuine, joyful and loving. Was it possible my Muslim people had gotten it wrong when it came to Christians?

Ilyas and I kept up our discussions. Often, they turned into debates. Sometimes, I grew angry. He gently tried to convince me to become a Christian, and I tried to convince him to become a Muslim. One day, Ilyas introduced me to a person who had graduated from Muhammad V University with a bachelor's degree in Islamic Studies. He was a Christian from a Muslim background. I sat down with the man, and we spent four hours debating about the godhead of Jesus Christ.

"Is Jesus really God's son?" I wanted to challenge him. This was not what I'd been taught, and I believed he was not.

"Yes, Jesus is God's son," he replied, and he sought to prove it with some verses from the Bible. He pointed out the verses that described the miracles of Jesus, including the resurrection of the dead, which only God could do.

I went home, feeling overwhelmed and confused. My safe Muslim world had been rocked, and I didn't know what to do.

Ilyas introduced me to his Christian friends. They met in a house on Saturday nights, playing piano and guitar and singing Christian songs. They were very kind and respectful to me, and I enjoyed hanging out with them. Soon, they became my true friends. But in the back of my mind, I held on to my agenda. *I need to convert these people to Islam. I will listen to them talk about their God and their religion, but I hope that they will eventually come to my side and see the truth.* I had won first prize in a debate on my faith in high school. If I could win such a prize, surely I could convert these Christian friends.

I went home and began studying the Bible, trying to find mistakes in it. *Surely, I will find some things that don't make sense. I will go back and prove to these people that I know the truth. They have it wrong, and I've got it right.*

The more I studied, the more I became convinced I needed to stand up for the truth about Islam. *Ilyas, his sister and their friends are so nice, and they certainly are not the type of Christians I expected to meet. I really enjoy their friendship. But I must convince them that they are wrong. Islam is the only way.*

I began thinking about writing an Arabic book, pointing out the mistakes in the Bible. *I will become the next Deedat. I will write a book that will cause Christians to convert. If I do convert them, God will grant me a great reward. This is what Islam teaches.*

Meanwhile, I continued going to the mosque for prayer, following every Islamic practice carefully. But I also kept hanging out with Ilyas and his Christian friends. While I continued to debate them, I also genuinely enjoyed their company. They welcomed me as one of their own and did not treat me any differently because of my faith. They introduced me to their Christian family and also to some American missionaries. I befriended the missionaries and found them to be warm and welcoming, too. As I watched their lives, I became impressed. *These are good people. They love their God, they love others and they love their community. They are not at all like I expected Christians to be.*

Ilyas and his family became friends of my family. They invited me over for Christmas dinner and also invited my family to weddings and other events. My family liked them well enough, as they treated us very respectfully. But I made sure to let my family know I had no interest in converting to Christianity. I even threw in the occasional joke about their Christian faith, just to assure my parents I wasn't leaning in another direction. *I am a Muslim,* I told myself adamantly. *It is okay to have Christian friends, but I am not going to convert to their faith.*

As time went by, however, my heart continued to shift. While I'd started out reading the Bible to convince myself of its errors, I began to read it for pleasure. I found myself intrigued by the God of the Bible. He seemed loving and kind. And his son, Jesus, seemed compassionate and loving as well. The New Testament told the story of Jesus' life and the many miracles he'd performed. Jesus healed the sick, prayed for the hurting and commanded his followers to love people, no matter their race, social status or affiliation. "I am the way, the truth and the life," Jesus said in the Bible.

Was this really possible? Was Jesus really God's son, as my Christian friends said? Or was this all a myth?

They have lost the truth. The words of my Muslim mentors echoed through my head every time I felt myself drawn toward this Jesus of the Bible. *Just remember, they have lost the truth. Islam is the only way.* This idea had been ingrained in me before I even touched my first soccer ball. My father's father was a descendant of the prophet Muhammad; we were practically Islamic royalty. To top it off, I was my parents' only son. I could never sway from what I'd been brought up to believe.

Or could I?

I graduated from high school and began attending classes at the university. The university was far from my home, and I had to take two separate buses to get there. I enjoyed my studies, but the minute I got home, I began reading the Bible, still intrigued by the Jesus I was learning about. My heart continued to shift, and the certainty I'd felt about my own religion now didn't seem quite as solid. I felt as if I was standing at a crossroads, facing two different paths. I could continue down the path I knew so well, the only path I'd followed my entire life. That path was comfortable and safe. I had memorized every detail of that path, never expecting to detour.

But another path now beckoned me to take a stroll, to explore what lay ahead. That path felt scary, because I'd never walked down it before. I also felt excited, convinced something wonderfully surprising might happen if I took a few steps forward.

On Fridays after class, I went over to Ilyas and Samia's house. Their mother welcomed me in the door and asked me to stay for dinner. She prepared a wonderful meal of Moroccan couscous, one of my favorite dishes. We sat around the table, laughing and talking. They exhibited such simplicity, wisdom and kindness, I could not help but be drawn to them.

Soon, they became like a second family. While my father spent most of his time working, Ilyas' father stepped in as another male role model. I enjoyed his company immensely.

Though Ilyas' family openly discussed their faith, they also let me discuss mine. Sometimes I shared something from the Quran, and they listened respectfully.

"That is a good point," they sometimes allowed when I'd finished explaining my views.

Yeah! I've convinced them of something! I felt excited at the idea of sharing my Muslim faith with them. But at the same time, I felt drawn to their Christian faith.

What is happening here? I've tried so hard to defend my faith, scouring the Bible for mistakes. But instead, I've only felt myself drawn to the Christian faith even more. Christian people are not at all what I thought they were. I've been told they don't have the truth, but is it possible I've been the one missing the truth all along?

I continued listening to and reading any Christian material I could get my hands on, including videotapes and books. The years passed, and I continued to search. Though I still followed through with my daily prayers at the mosque, I no longer felt convinced I knew the truth. In fact, I felt more drawn to Christianity than ever. By the end of my fourth year of study and comparison, I felt less sure about Islam than I ever had.

One thing in particular began to trouble me. I began asking the question, "If I were to die today, would I go to be with God in heaven?" I began questioning the prophet Muhammad. According to the Islamic religion, followers of Prophet Muhammad were not sure they would go to heaven when they died, even if they adhered to the best ethics and did everything right. Even Abu Bakr al-Siddiq and Umar ibn al-Khattab, the most influential Muslim Caliphs and the very close friends to Prophet Muhammad, were not sure where they would go after they died. The idea of not knowing frightened me terribly.

All this time, I've assumed I'm going to heaven when I die, but what if I don't? If Abu Bakr and Umar, two of the most influential leaders in the Islamic faith, were not sure about their own fate, how can I be sure about mine? I could pray, fast and even go to Mecca, but at the end of my life, I am still not guaranteed eternity in heaven. Can this be right?

I asked my Muslim friends, including some Imams, about this idea.

"Only God knows for sure where we will end up when we die," they said with a shrug.

Their answer didn't bring me any comfort. I turned back to the Bible and continued studying it. I began to learn about the concept of grace, the idea of receiving something you don't deserve. I read Ephesians 2:8, which stated, "For it is by grace you have been saved, through faith — and this is not from yourselves, it is the gift of God." I read the passage over and over, intrigued. *Wow. Is it possible grace is the way to heaven, not good works?*

The more I mulled over the idea of grace, the more I became convinced Christianity must be the truth. *This is so simple. I do not need to earn God's love by partaking in certain rituals or praying certain prayers every day. If I simply trust him with my heart, as the Bible says, I can receive his grace and spend eternity with him in heaven. This sounds almost too good to be true, but I think I believe it. In fact, I think I was created for God and Christianity.*

I stopped going to the mosque every day. My mother took notice.

"Why aren't you going to the mosque to pray, Halim?" she asked.

"I have been too busy with my studies," I said casually.

I continued coming up with excuses as to why I could not attend the mosque. Meanwhile, I kept praying a simple prayer, "God, show me the truth. I want to know the truth."

Next, I confided in a close Christian friend. "I am seeking God and seeking the truth," I told him. "He is changing my heart about Christianity."

"When you pray, pray in Jesus' name," he encouraged me.

"Okay, I'll do that," I agreed.

One night, I turned off all the lights in my room and climbed into bed. "God, I am so confused," I prayed.

"Please show me the truth! Help me make a decision about my faith. Show me if I am supposed to be a Christian. In Jesus' name, amen."

I drifted off into a deep sleep. In the middle of the night, I had a dream. In that dream, I saw Jesus. I saw him clearly — his colorful robe, his kind eyes as he beckoned me forward. "Follow me," he said gently. He spoke in a different language, but I understood him clearly.

I awoke, my heart thudding as I replayed the dream in my mind. It had been so vivid, as if Jesus himself had been standing before me in real life. *What was that all about?*

Perhaps this is Satan trying to deceive me, I told myself. But Prophet Muhammad had said that if we saw him or one of the other prophets in a dream, it was the truth. I quickly grabbed my Quran and started reading it. I tried to shake off the dream.

But I could not shake it off. I had seen Jesus clearly, and he had asked me to follow him.

The next morning, I visited one of my Christian friends and told him about my dream.

"You have to make a decision," he said. "You are not the only one who has seen Jesus in a dream." He gave me an Arabic book titled *The Children of Ishmael,* which was filled with many stories of other Middle Eastern people who had also seen Jesus in a dream.

"Thank you, I'll read it," I told him.

I read the book, intrigued by the stories, so similar to mine. In my heart, I knew I wanted to be a Christian. *I now believe this is the truth. But Islam is so ingrained in me. And what will my family and friends think if they learn I've converted to Christianity? This could cause a huge division — an earthquake even! Our family is Muslim. It is the way things have always been. I would be the first to shake things up. Could I really do that to the ones I love the most?*

I knew I faced great risk by making the leap to Christianity. But I also knew what I had to do. My heart told me the truth. I wanted to follow Jesus Christ and the one true God of the Bible. I was ready to take the next step and denounce my Islamic faith, no matter the cost.

God, please come into my heart and life, I prayed. *I have been seeking you, asking for the truth, and I feel you have given it to me. I want to follow Jesus. I want to live a new life. And I want to spend eternity in heaven with you. I believe that it is only through your grace and your son, Jesus, that I can experience new life in you. So I ask you for that. I confess the wrong things I've done. Please make me new. From this moment on, I am yours.*

I took my Islamic books and anything else representing Islam and burned them all on the rooftop of my house. I stopped going to the mosque and also stopped talking about the Muslim religion. *I am not Muslim anymore. I am a Christian.* I repeated this over and over to myself, a mixture of fear and excitement washing over me. I had discovered what I believed to be the absolute truth, and I wanted to shout it for all to hear. But I also knew my decision came with great consequence. When my family discovered what I'd done, they might possibly shun me forever. *The road ahead feels scary, but I will face it with courage. I have God on my side.*

I began sharing Christianity with others at the university, telling them about the simple, beautiful message of grace. I gave Arabic Bibles to some of my classmates as well. The dean, along with the department head, learned what I'd done and called me in for a closed meeting. They asked me if I'd become a Christian, and I innocently replied yes.

"You are not saved by your good works," I told them excitedly, hoping to convert them to Christianity, too. "Jesus died on the cross for our sins. Through him, we can be forgiven. He was the perfect sacrifice."

But the dean and the department head did not appreciate my attempt to convert them. Instead, they grew angry. "That will be enough!" they barked.

The next day, the department head opened his morning session with a warning for all students. "There is someone in the classroom who is trying to share the Bible with other students. You should be careful."

He then singled me out and began humiliating me in front of my peers.

"Every Muslim converted to Christianity is someone who has received money and advantages from a Christian organization. Do not pay them any attention," he said.

A few days later, I learned that the dean wrote a report to the Ministry of Interior about my behavior. Seventeen students signed the report as witnesses that I'd talked to them about Christianity. A few days after that, the police showed up at my house, looking for me. They didn't find me there, but they interrogated my father for two hours.

Next, the police came looking for me at the university. "We'd like to meet for coffee and discuss a few things," they said.

I agreed to meet with them, remembering not to divulge too much.

"Why are you Christian now? What do you think about Prophet Muhammad?" The police fired questions at me, and I answered politely but vaguely. I knew someone in my family had talked to them about my new faith, and they wanted to pin me down and vilify me as much as possible. Because I was young, however, they let me go without further questions.

I went to one of my classmates and asked him to tell me about the letter that the dean sent to the Ministry of Interior and that my peers had signed. "I'd like to know; please tell me," I told him.

He reluctantly told me what happened. My heart sank as I listened to him. *My classmates turned on me. I have become an outcast around here, and now I'm being treated like I'm a criminal! I need to stay strong in my faith and stick close to my Christian friends, because things are about to get rough.*

In April of my final year at the university, I decided to get baptized to profess my new faith. I had been attending a Bible study at a local Christian church, and an Egyptian-American pastor baptized me, dunking me under water in front of my friends. It was a wonderful moment I'd never forget. As I emerged from the water, I glanced around at all the smiling faces, the people who supported me and my decision. *I am not sure how the rest of the world will respond to my decision, but I know I have a family here in this church.*

It didn't take long for my family to realize what was going on. One night, at 3 a.m., my mother tiptoed into my room and woke me up. "I have one question for you. Answer me yes or no."

I rubbed the sleep from my eyes, knowing full well what came next. My heart began to race, and I braced myself for the interrogation.

"Someone told me you became a Christian. Is this true?" she demanded.

"Who told you this?"

"It doesn't matter who told me. Just answer the question. Is it true?"

I could not deny the truth. "Yes," I whispered. "It is true."

"Noooo!" My mother stood up and started to bang her head against the wall, rocking back and forth as she wailed. I jumped out of bed and tried to stop her, but she carried on, rocking and wailing as though someone had just died.

"I only have one son, and he is going to hell!" she screamed.

My father ran into the room to see what all the commotion was about.

"Your son has become a Christian!" my mother cried.

My father whipped around to face me. "Is this true?"

I nodded, my heart still racing wildly.

"Leave this home immediately, and do not come back unless you return to Islam. Do you understand?"

I did not try to argue. I had known this day might come. I grabbed a few belongings, brushed past my parents and headed out the front door and into the night. The cold whipped at my cheeks as I began to walk. I could not get my mother's screams out of my head. I knew I had broken her heart and greatly disappointed both her and my father. How could I carry on our lineage if I was no longer a Muslim? The idea that I'd divided our family devastated me. But at the same time, I firmly believed I'd found the truth. I could not turn around now.

I walked for nearly two hours, ending up on the doorstep of my friend Ayman's house. He opened the door in his pajamas, surprised to see me. "Halim! What are you doing here?"

"My parents found out I am a Christian and asked me to leave the house," I explained. "May I stay with you?"

"Of course."

Ayman let me in. "Hallelujah!" he said when I told him the story. "Satan was trying to keep your faith hidden, but now your family knows, and may God use you to bring them to him! This is great news! We don't want to wake up the family, so go to sleep, and we can talk about this later." He helped me to bed, and I fell back asleep.

The next morning, Ayman shared my story with his parents.

"Would you like me to go to your father and talk to him?" his father asked.

"That's okay. I think I should call them, though, so they don't worry." I called my parents to let them know I'd be staying with Ayman. After a few days, I returned home, hoping to work things out with my parents.

To my horror and dismay, my father had not cooled down. On the contrary, he was angrier than ever. "You are not welcome in this house anymore," he said adamantly. "I have checked your documents and seen that you recently visited Egypt. I am wondering who paid for your flight since you are only a senior at the university and do not have any income of your own."

I started to protest and explain that I had to attend a training that related to my study, while the reality was something else. I had attended training for the future leaders in Kasr El Dobara Church in Cairo, Egypt.

"You are a varmint, nothing but vile," he spat out. "Get out of my house!"

I left the house for the second time. Ilyas invited me to stay with him and his parents for the next month. I took them up on the offer, grateful for their hospitality. They treated me like a son, offering dinners and a warm bed to sleep in.

After a month with Ilyas' family, I returned home, and this time, my parents received me much differently. My mother convinced my father to give me a chance, and they brought an Imam in to talk to me instead of kicking me out of the house.

The Imam, who led prayer at the mosque, tried talking me out of my decision, but I politely told him I'd already made up my mind. I was a Christian now.

In July, I graduated from the university. Because of the report the police had filed following the investigation, I could not find a job. Word had spread quickly around town, and everyone knew I'd turned away from Islam. I began working with a missionary in a school of languages in Fes, and we then opened a branch in Rabat. I taught Arabic to the missionaries and enjoyed the position thoroughly. After a few months, I became the director of the school, and I began to train other teachers.

In January two years later, I had the opportunity to participate in a sports outreach in Bamako, Mali, during the Africa Cup of Nations. Because of my soccer background, I was selected to play on the national team U17, which I considered a true honor. I spent two weeks in Bamako. Famous Christian African soccer players joined us for the outreach, and we shared our Christian faith with many people. After one of the messages, I had the chance to talk with a Muslim man. I shared my story with him — how I'd begun as a skeptic but had chosen to follow Christ, despite the opposition.

"It is only by God's grace that we can get to heaven," I told the young man. "There is nothing we can do to earn God's love. Good works are not enough."

"I would like to be a Christian like you!" the young man said, his eyes lighting up.

We prayed right then and there, and the man invited

Jesus Christ into his life and heart, just as I had. I was ecstatic. *Thank you, God, for using me to reach someone else! I pray you will use me to reach many more people for you!*

That July, I received an invitation to be a part of an intensive three-month training program with International Sports Leadership School. The school was started in 1999 after the International Sports Coalition realized the increasing importance of training a new generation of leaders in sports ministry.

Every year, leaders from different countries went to South Africa for a three-month training course. Each class consisted of roughly 30 leaders from 20 different cultures. Because of my soccer background, my faith and my desire for outreach, I was considered an ideal candidate.

I spent the next three months learning about 10 different strategies on how to use sports to proclaim the good news of Jesus Christ. While I was there, the police returned to my parents' house and asked them about my travel. They also investigated Ilyas and asked him about our relationship. One thing had become clear: The Moroccan government was on to me. Because of my decision to follow Christ, I was considered a threat. My decision to abandon Islam had been taken quite seriously, and if I continued doing what I was doing, I could face serious consequences.

The following summer, I was hired as an Arabic teacher in an American school in Morocco. After a few years, they hired me for the position of personnel administrator in human resources. I enjoyed the strong Christian leadership there and felt right at home with both the teachers and the students. Though we could not openly talk about Jesus in the classroom, I had plenty of opportunities to share Jesus with the high school students, as well as the faculty and administrative staff.

I wanted to support my family, so I tried giving them a portion of my paycheck each month. My parents, however, refused the money.

"If it is coming from a Christian, I cannot accept it," my mom said.

Her choice saddened me, but I knew I could not do anything else. I had no intention of turning back to Islam, no matter how difficult things became.

I continued spending time with Ilyas and Samia. I had grown fond of Samia and asked for her hand in marriage. In our culture, we did not date but rather committed ourselves to be wed. Samia got a job at the same school, working as a kindergarten assistant.

After a four-month engagement, we married at our pastor's home in November 2003. I invited my entire family to attend, but my mother talked my sisters out of coming. They cried, along with my mother, and none of them came. My father attended, however, along with nearly 200 other guests. As they took their seats under a large outdoor tent, I noticed two policemen walking by, as well as a police van parked next to the house.

The government is watching us. They know a large group of Christians are gathering today, and they are still investigating me. I must be careful, but I will not let their presence dampen my excitement.

Our pastor performed the ceremony, which included a time of prayer and worship. It was unlike any Muslim wedding I'd ever attended.

"I like that pastor," my father said after the ceremony ended.

Wow, God! That's a huge step for my father! Thank you for bringing him here today!

Though I wished the rest of my family had been there to see me wed my bride, it was still one of the best days of my life, second only to the day I invited Jesus into my heart.

The following year, I began serving as a volunteer coordinator for the International Sports Coalition in North Africa. I believed God shaped my life and my skills to start training leaders from North Africa about sports ministry. Because I was an active member in the church and also played soccer professionally, the leadership selected me for the position. As with the opportunity to serve in the major sports events around the world, I considered the position a great honor. I felt like God continued opening doors for me to share my faith everywhere I went. While this all felt very exciting, it felt scary as well. Not only had my decision to follow Christ shaken things up in my own home, but it had shaken up things in my larger community as well. And the storm that had been brewing was about to turn into a full-blown tornado, one that would rock my world like never before.

భాఁ భాఁ భాఁ

Samia gave birth to our first child, a son. That same year, the police investigated three church leaders about the sports ministry training I had arranged for people from Tunisia, Algeria, Mauritania and Morocco. *How did they know about the training?* I wondered, shocked. *And why did they not come to me directly?*

I wondered if the police had listened in on our phone calls or if someone from the church had been pressured to tell them. Not wanting to put anyone in danger, I cancelled the invitation for the people from Algeria and Mauritania, limited the number of participants and changed the meeting place out of concern for the security of the attendees.

One thing was becoming evident: The Moroccan government did not like Christians. They sought to put a stop to anyone who professed a Christian faith. Because my wife and I were Christians, we faced great danger. Could we stay in the country and keep doing what we were doing, knowing we put our lives on the line?

Three years later, my wife gave birth to another child, a little girl. We continued working at the same school, teaching. Things kept heating up, however.

The Moroccan government began confiscating passports of active Moroccan Christians, and when I submitted an application and tried to start an official sports association to serve the kids in Morocco, I never received an answer back. I also learned that several people who had joined my Moroccan Christian Facebook group were just Muslims posing as Christians. Some of them were attending the home church that I was leading in my house, trying to garner information. I felt like a character in a suspense movie, always looking over my shoulder to make sure no one was stalking me. *I cannot live in peace anymore. I don't know what to do.*

When my grandmother passed away, I went to my aunt's house for the funeral. There, I met up with my cousin, who belonged to the Islamic Salafist Group in Morocco.

"Can we go up to my room on the roof? I need to talk to you about something important," he said to me.

We headed up to his room, and to my surprise, four bearded men suddenly appeared. My cousin introduced me to one of the men. "He is an expert in debates with Christians and would like to talk to you," he said.

"I don't think this is the right time," I said calmly. "I need to go see some people from my family who I haven't seen in a long time." I began backing away, but the men did not.

"Where does Jesus say in the Bible that he is God?" the man demanded.

I refused to answer. The guy charged toward me and grabbed my neck, yanking the collar of my jacket. "You should be killed!" he screamed.

"Stop it!" my cousin interjected. "Let's talk to him first and see if maybe he will be willing to come back to Islam."

At that moment, someone knocked on the door,

asking for help setting up chairs. "I'll help you!" I cried, prying myself free from the guy's grip.

"Just know that if we hear that you evangelized someone, you will be killed!" he called after me.

I raced down the stairs, my heart thudding with every step. From that moment on, I feared for my life. Every time I walked down the street, I glanced back, expecting someone to be racing after me. I no longer felt safe in the country I'd been born in.

I am the outsider now. They treat me like a criminal, watching my every move, interrogating me, threatening me because I will not convert back to Islam. I will not back down in my faith, but I do not want to put my family in danger.

The same year my grandma passed away, the Moroccan government led a fierce campaign against Moroccan Christians and missionaries in Morocco. One of the American teachers at the school I worked at was accused of telling the kids about Jesus. She prayed and encouraged one of the middle school students to become a Christian, and he did. His father learned of his decision and grew so upset that he hired one of the best lawyers in the country. His lawyer and the Islamic political party to which he belonged led a huge campaign that made the front page of newspapers and magazines everywhere. Even TV news anchors discussed the scandal.

The police investigated many employees in my school about the proselytizing, and the investigations led investigators to discover the secret Christian orphanage where many expat staff visited often to serve orphans. The investigation ended up with the deportation of 140 missionaries, mostly Americans, and they closed the orphanage and expelled the employees.

The following September, many Moroccan newspapers published a report leaked by WikiLeaks. The report detailed the meeting that another Moroccan church leader and I had with a representative of International Religious Freedom. We made statements about the persecution of the minority of Moroccan Christians and the government's responsibility for it.

This coincided with the victory of the Islamic brotherhood party PJD in the elections to become the official ruling party in November 2011, creating a state of anticipation in the country. Everybody asked how the Islamists would deal with different issues, and we as Christians faced fear, because we knew that the new government would raise the level of persecution.

The police interrogated me and my Christian friend about what we shared in the document that WikiLeaks published. "We think you and other Christian leaders are trying to form a minority of Christians to shake the monarchy system in our country," they accused.

They asked us to not leave the country and to be ready any time they needed further information.

One Sunday morning, the police showed up at my house. I went out to talk to them.

"Halim, we would like to talk to you at a coffee shop," they said.

"I've told you before, if you want to investigate me, you need to bring official documents," I said firmly.

They continued to interrogate me, however. I tried to convince them we did not have an agenda, but they did not believe me. At last, they let me go.

My parents and everybody in my extended family knew about the WikiLeaks document because my full name was mentioned on that report, so they considered me a traitor who not only converted to Christianity, but was one of the church leaders who had an "agenda." Of course, they were quite sure that I shared the Gospel with others.

"We are not safe here anymore," I told my wife. "The Moroccan government is not going to back down. As Christians, we are the minority. I think we may need to leave the country."

We had tried to be patient, staying in our country to show the love of Jesus to our families, friends and neighbors. But the pressure had taken a psychological toll on me. My blood pressure began to skyrocket, and I had trouble sleeping. In May 2013, we learned that Morocco's highest authority had issued a fatwa, calling for the execution of any Muslim who left his Islamic faith. I knew what we had to do. Though it would mean starting over somewhere far away, saying goodbye to the only place I'd ever known and leaving my family roots, I knew we needed to leave. If we did not, we might all die.

ॐॐॐ

In August 2013, my wife and I sought asylum to the United States, petitioning to find refuge in another country because of our persecution. I came first, and then my wife and children followed in December. I hired a lawyer and followed all the procedures to begin making a new life for ourselves. We settled in Austin, Texas, but without a social security number, I had a difficult time finding someone to rent us a house.

We came with only the clothes on our backs, leaving behind everything we knew. We did not have jobs, did not know anyone and did not know how we'd pay the bills. We had officially lost all our belongings, having sold our furniture, cars and everything else we owned. But I knew just what we needed to help us get back on our feet. We needed to find a church.

We visited GTaustin and fell in love with it right away. The people welcomed us in as though they'd known us forever. And the pastor, Kermit, treated us with the utmost kindness and respect. When the church folks learned of our situation, they stepped in to help in any way they could. Before long, we felt ourselves right at home.

I told Pastor Kermit about my high blood pressure and how I'd had to take medication after going through such stress. He suggested we pray for my health. We did, and that night, I decided to stop taking my medication. When I went to monitor my blood pressure the next day, I discovered it was better than when I'd been on my meds!

"God healed me! Your prayers worked!" I told Pastor Kermit excitedly.

I joined a fitness center to keep in shape, and we enrolled the children in school. I began volunteering as a soccer coach, and my wife volunteered in the children's ministry at church.

Because we hadn't received work permits yet, we could not find jobs. We went through many financial crises. We rarely shared our needs with others.

We just prayed to God and every time were provided with an opportunity to do some unofficial work for extra cash.

"This is part of our faith journey," I told my wife. "This is where God steps in to provide."

We continued to trust in God. When it came time to pay the rent, we trusted in God to take care of it. We continued the process of asylum and hoped one day to be official American citizens. I talked to my family by phone here and there. God softened my mother's heart, and she no longer felt animosity toward me regarding my faith.

In the meantime, we enjoyed our wonderful church GTaustin. It's been a great spiritual protection for us. Pastor Kermit and everyone became like family to us. We prayed for each other, studied the Bible together and helped each other when needs arose. I do not know what I would have done without our church family. They were a lifeline for us in the midst of uncertain circumstances.

I often think back to that classroom encounter in high school, when I met my wife for the first time. Little did I know that moment would change the course of my life, as I began to question Islam and seek out Christianity. My road has been difficult, and I have even feared for my life, but I would not change a thing.

I've been so grateful I found Jesus and, most importantly, that I found grace. There was nothing I could do to earn God's love, I learned. I simply trusted in him, one day at a time. I not only found freedom in a new country, but I found freedom in Christ. And that was the best feeling of all.

THE SON OF A FAULTED FATHER
The Story of Dwayne
Written by Ameerah Collins

I'll never be good enough. It doesn't matter how hard I try. He'll never be satisfied.

I looked at my father swabbing the wet cement. Absentmindedly, I handed him tools to level the cement. I listened to him drone on about the significance of money, status and future career. Everything was about power to him. If you didn't have power, you didn't have anything.

That's all he cares about. He doesn't love me for me. He doesn't care about anything.

I tugged at my slacks and dropped to my knees beside my father. I swiped at the cement, hurriedly spreading it, and nodded at my father's words.

"You're going to have to be someone great if you want to be a valued man in this family, boy. If you don't hold a leadership position in this community, you'll be nothing in my eyes. If you don't get your education and land a high-paying job, you'll be nothing to me. You understand?"

If I don't meet your expectations, you'll look down on me. Yeah, I understand.

"Yeah. I got it, Dad."

ৡৡৡ

Growing up, I never established the solid connection with my father that I always wanted. He came from a Spanish Basque culture with many powerful men in his family. In our part of Texas, you either respected and adored the men in my family or you hated everything about them. That reputation dated back to my father's father, a Mexican gangster in the 1920s. The man was a ruthless bootlegger and train robber. People feared him. Just hearing about my grandfather explained so much about my father. It's as if Dad was destined to turn out just as ruthless.

Dad wore a tough exterior, which seemed to wrap around his stubborn heart. He was a racist man, who had a low tolerance for black people and Anglos. "He wasn't always so unloving and hateful," my big brother once said. "At one point, he was kind and approachable. You were just a baby, though. You wouldn't have remembered him like that."

Apparently, the Korean War left something evil in him. I tried to believe my dad was once a good guy, but all I knew was the stone-faced man with the hardened demeanor. The Marine who just couldn't shake the horror he'd seen overseas. A father who couldn't love his children the way he should have.

I don't believe he truly loved Mom, either. I never understood why. She was so sweet, fun and possessed a nurturing touch that just tugged my siblings and me toward her. My father had this way of suppressing her, though. Mom knew he was an unfaithful man, but she didn't leave him. When I was 5 years old, I realized he didn't deserve her.

A door slammed, heavy footsteps followed and a chair scrapped against the floor. Even from another room, I could picture my father plopping down on the chair and slumping over the kitchen table with Mom bustling around in the kitchen, trying to keep busy.

"Where have you been now, Marcos?" My mother's irate tone reached my bedroom.

"What are you talking about, woman?" Dad slurred. "I've been out drinking with the guys. Where the hell else would I be?"

"Drinking with the guys, huh? Yeah. You're a real drunk, all right." She laughed sharply. "And a *liar*. A *cheat*. You took me away from everything! From my family, my church! And for what? For this unhappy life? You're not the man I married! If I'd known you'd be like this —"

"Gwen, stop," he warned.

"NO!" she shrieked, and I flinched at the crack in her voice. "I'M NOT STUPID!"

"Then stop acting like it! Shut your mouth talking to me like that!"

"Do you think I'm crazy? I know you're with other women, Marcos. I just know it! You come home reeking of them, and you don't even have the decency to care! You don't care! You don't care about me, you don't care about anything. You're a horrible example for your boys!"

"SHUT UP, GWEN!" Dad bellowed, and she didn't say another word. "I don't have time for your insecurities! I'm not cheating on you. Just shut up before you wake my kids."

She scoffed between soft sobs. "Oh, please, Marcos. Like you care."

My siblings and I found out Dad cheated on Mom so often that he ended up having several other families. It was nothing for us to bump into our half-brothers and sisters around town. Kids claimed to be my father's children all the time, and we knew they weren't lying. Sometimes we shared the same last name and even physical features.

When I was about 10, Dad's control over Mom became more powerful and evident. He called himself a Catholic man, but he never stepped foot in church. He forced us to attend church every Sunday, even though he never went. Mom was a Protestant, yet he forbade her to go to those types of churches. Not only did he ostracize Mom from her family by moving to a town where most people spoke Spanish, but he also took away her closeness with her own church.

I saw how badly that hurt her, and I hated seeing her hurt.

Dad also sent us to a Catholic school. We learned special prayers and memorized verses from the Bible, but I never felt like I was actually getting to know God as an actual being. Once, the school invited a speaker to discuss the importance of God. His speech was different from the priests, though. He spoke about giving your life to Jesus and truly leaning on him. The man actually seemed to have a message from God. His words intrigued me.

What does it mean to accept salvation? How does one give his life to Jesus? Why don't I hear talk like this from anyone else at my Catholic church or school? I didn't really get it, but his words stuck with me throughout my childhood and adolescence.

At this time, my grandfather on my mother's side mailed me religious tracts. They were pieces of paper or small pamphlets that focused on the teachings of Jesus. I usually tossed them in my desk drawer without reading them, but the speaker at school made me think of the tracts and my grandfather. I believed Grandpa knew my dad cut us off from seeing Mom's side of the family, so he used those tracts as a sense of encouragement and hope for us.

As I thought about my grandfather and the speaker's words, I found myself wondering what it was like to have a real connection with God. I was so used to structure, following traditions and being bored out of my mind sitting in church. I wanted something more. I loved my father, but I didn't want to grow up and become a hardened man like him. I wanted to have the traits of my grandpa and have the sort of outlook on God that speaker from school had.

I didn't know how to acquire all that. I didn't even believe I could.

෧෧෧

As a teenager, my mindset shifted. I still had a gentle heart and wanted to be a man like my grandpa, but I didn't consider that to be realistic as long as my father was *my father.* So, like Dad, I started drinking. One time my cousin and I were driving while intoxicated, and we got pulled over. Because of our last name, the officer let us off. I should have been thrown in jail or at least tattled on to my father, but none of that happened. I couldn't believe it.

Over the years, it became clear to my siblings and me that Dad's acceptance of us depended on how well we performed academically and athletically. I didn't make the best grades, but I was a good athlete. He loved that about me.

During the summers, Dad made my brothers and me work for his construction company laying down concrete instead of hanging out with our friends. He wanted us to realize we needed a stable career in order to be anyone special in life. Our security as men, he stressed, depended on status, money and anything else that revolved around power and control.

"You're nothing without a good profession, Dwayne." Dad held one end of a metal straightedge while I held the other. We slid it against the wet cement, leveling it, as I listened to him. "Your uncles and I, we all have solid jobs. Our family name is respected in this town. If you're not like us, you might as well change your last name."

I sighed. It was always the same old thing with him — money and power. "I'm going to be someone you can be proud of, Dad. You don't have to worry. I understand."

"Don't be a thick head! It's not just about me being proud of you," he scolded. "This is about your upholding of the family name. Your mother is Anglo," he scoffed. "You don't want to be associated with that. You're a Spanish Basque. A Basque has power. A Basque has money. You got that?"

"Yeah, I got it." I flung the metal straightedge aside and grabbed two hand float tools to even the surface out a bit more. Dad eyed me with doubt as I handed him the object.

"You're going to have to be someone great if you want to be a valued man in this family, boy. If you don't hold a leadership position in this community, you'll be nothing in my eyes. If you don't get your education and land a high-paying job, you'll be nothing to me. You understand?"

If I don't meet your expectations, you'll look down on me. Yeah, I understand.

I nodded my head as insecurity flooded through me. Dad didn't care about pursuing a career that involved helping people or caring for those who needed it, he just cared about the money. If I aspired to be a lawyer, proving the innocent as such wouldn't be his primary concern, only winning the case. If I wanted to be a professor, he wouldn't care about how many students I helped, he was just interested in how prestigious the institution I taught at would be.

I wanted a career in which I helped people, especially children. I wanted to do something that made a difference in the lives of others. I wanted to reach out to people in a way that my father didn't understand. Over time, I accepted it didn't matter what I wanted to be in life.

I just needed to make sure Dad approved of me. If he didn't, it would tear me apart.

᪥᪥᪥

By the time I graduated high school, I was ready to escape the controlling ways my father ruled the household. I'd met a girl named Pamela, and I wanted to start my life with her. She became pregnant while we were in college, and we really didn't know what to do. We were two youngsters who'd messed up pretty royally. I didn't want people looking at Pamela a certain way because we weren't married, so we talked to our friends about it.

"Well, you guys are so young," our friends said. "You haven't even finished college yet. What will your parents think? Maybe you should consider abortion."

"I don't want an abortion," Pamela insisted when we were alone. "That's just, it's just wrong. People try to desensitize it by saying it's just a termination, but it's more than that."

"I know." I nodded and reached for her hand. "It's killing your own child."

"I don't want an abortion." Pamela's hair whipped as she shook her head. "It's sick. I don't want to do it, Dwayne."

"Good," I breathed with a small smile. "It'll be hard,

sweetheart, but we'll get through this. I'm going to work hard for us. We're going to raise our baby and go to school at the same time. It's the only choice we have."

Pamela and I planned a shotgun wedding with our family and close friends. Just a few months later, she gave birth to our daughter Alessandra. I excelled in college and worked hard in postgraduate school. Part of my hard work was because I still harbored a desire to please my father and uncles. I didn't want to be the only man in the family without a high-profile position or high salary. I couldn't afford to fail them. The other reason I worked so hard was for Pamela and Alessandra. I wanted to give them a good life and show everyone that although we were a young couple with a baby, we could make it.

Dad made frequent visits during my postgraduate school years, but usually the visits were rather stressful. I constantly worried about his approval. I still found him unapproachable and hard to talk to, but one day I decided to give it a shot, anyway. I was older and thought maybe I could talk to him like a man and not a boy.

We were driving downtown, and he spotted a black man walking on the sidewalk.

"There goes that nigger." Dad pointed at the man and sneered. "Just look at him."

I sighed and shook my head. "That's horrible, Dad. What's the problem with a black guy walking down the street? He's not bothering anyone. You shouldn't call him the n-word. Just call him a black man."

"Just call him a black man?" Dad's voice heightened.

"Are you crazy? Now that's terrible. Why would I call him a black man when he's a nigger?"

"Well, yeah." I glanced at him. "I mean, you don't know anything about that man. You're using that nasty word on him because of the color of his skin. It's hateful of you."

"It's not hateful," Dad spat. "It's just the truth. He is what he is. You'd do right to accept that, Dwayne."

"What if someone hated you because of your skin color? You have dark skin, too. How would you like it if someone called you a spic? Wouldn't that hurt you?"

"WHAT?" He exploded. "HOW DARE YOU USE THAT WORD ON ME!"

"I'm not using it on you," I quickly explained. "I'm just saying it's the same thing. You calling black people the n-word and folks calling you spic. They are both racial slurs."

The rest of Dad's visit didn't go so well. He chewed me out in the car and didn't take my comparison of the two words very well. I knew then that would be my last time addressing any issues with him. After all those years, he still wasn't an approachable man. He still wasn't the father I wanted him to be. He still hadn't changed.

I believed only God could change him.

❧❧❧

Pamela and I had more children. Periodically, I'd gather the pile of tracts I'd collected from my grandfather throughout my youth and read them. We still considered ourselves Catholic, but we only went to church on Easter. My only connection to God came from those tracts. After reading them every now and then, I started to feel like I needed more of God.

Just like when I was a boy in sixth grade and that guest speaker visited my school, I wanted to know what it really felt like to have that special link with God. I wanted to know what it meant to accept Jesus into your life. I had my own struggles and demons I was facing on the job. The hectic hours and emotional baggage that came with my career did nothing to ease my stress. I knew I needed help.

During one of my evening shifts, I turned the radio on to the Christian station. A speaker by the name of Billy Graham was talking about Jesus. His message sounded full of power and passion. It was nothing like what I'd ever heard at church. This man seemed to be extremely serious about God. He talked about how Jesus died and rose again, so we could follow him to heaven one day. I listened to him say I didn't need to handle my struggles on my own, not when I had a God in heaven who could solve all my problems. Billy Graham touched on forgiveness, giving your life to Jesus and developing that close relationship with God.

I was 32 years old, and I wanted God to save me from myself. To give me that love I needed. I knew I'd always had a void within me, derived from my father, and nothing seemed to ever fill it. That emptiness followed me through my childhood and skipped right on into my adulthood. I wanted to rid myself of those insecurities. The feelings of not being good enough had to go. The ache from never having a father who truly loved me for me. I just didn't want to feel that anymore.

I walked toward an empty room at my workplace and dropped to my knees. I kneeled before a chair, clasped my hands and bowed my head to God.

"God, please save me. I know I haven't been a great son to you. I've been so unfaithful, but I always knew you were there. I never followed the Bible or tried to really connect with you, even when I felt you pushing me to do so."

I fell apart before God, and I knew he heard my cries to him. I thought about all the times I abused alcohol and acted out because I couldn't deal with my father's expectations and open cruelty. I thought of his faithfulness to me. There were times when I should have landed myself in jail for being reckless and wild, but that hadn't happened. I thought it was because of my last name, but I supposed it was really due to God looking out for me. I just didn't realize it until years later.

I committed my life to God that evening. I wanted him to take control of my living and put me on the right path. I didn't want to become dependent upon alcohol like my father. I didn't want to turn into a mean man with horrible viewpoints like him. I wanted to be the best husband I possibly could be for Pamela. No way would I treat her the way Dad treated Mom.

As I continued to listen to more talks by Billy Graham

on the radio, I learned so much about Jesus that I'd never even heard of before. Unlike my father, God offered me gifts without expectation. God offered me *Jesus*, his own son, as a free gift. There were absolutely no strings attached to accepting Jesus into my heart. I didn't need to excel in every aspect of my life. God didn't expect me to never fall or screw up. I found it remarkable how Jesus took me as I was, marked up and blemished, and had no problem loving me.

I also realized that *God* found *me*. So many people talked about how they found God, but I really felt like God reached down from heaven and rescued me from a life of self-torment. I knew he'd always been there since the very beginning, but for so long I'd felt like an unstable, unsure, unloved son who couldn't please his father. God picked me up from my knees. He declared himself as my heavenly father — the one who loved me before I was even born.

When I gave my life to Jesus and told Pamela about what happened to me, she did the same thing. We became so determined to live the right way. Although we still didn't dedicate much time to our Catholic church, we started going more often. We also made sure to tune into the Christian radio station and felt like we received good teachings about Jesus from there.

One day we heard a local pastor teaching on the radio from a church called GTaustin. He spoke a great and fevered message from the Bible, and we decided to visit. As we sat in the pews and listened to that same speaker, we were transfixed by his words. The upbeat songs of praise that voiced such love and devotion toward God intrigued us. We hadn't heard music like that before. Unlike at our Catholic church, we didn't want to leave early or become bored during the service. Heck, we stayed on the edge of our seats and hung on to every word he said.

"So many of us have an urge to do good in this world." The pastor flipped through his Bible from the podium. "We have teachers, doctors, officers and lawmen all working toward helping the people. But we have to understand who we're helping these people for."

I looked at Pamela and raised my brow, wondering where he was going.

"Your good deeds toward others don't mean much to God, if you're just doing it to exalt yourself. If you're not doing good in God's name, then your mission is flawed, my brothers and sisters. If you want to be that esteemed leader in your community who everyone looks up to, then you are nothing but a boastful man or woman. You can't please God with an air of haughtiness hovering above you."

Wow, I thought to myself. *My father was wrong all along. It's not about prestige, power, money and status. It's about pleasing God and helping his people. It has nothing to do with me.*

"I urge you to do better in the Lord. Let everything you do be done for Jesus Christ. Don't help others to be seen by man. Don't behave in a manner in which people cannot see the light of Jesus within you." He spoke with such passion as people in the audience waved their hands and agreed with his words through head nods and shouts. "Don't just come to church on Sunday morning and not apply the Bible's teachings to your everyday life. What sense does that make? Let your life exemplify God. And you're not just doing this to build your relationship with God, but you're doing this so you can lead others to Christ, too."

I want people to see me and know I have God in my heart. I don't want to do anything else in my life for my own selfish reasons. I want to lead others to Christ.

After visiting GTaustin, we couldn't stay away. Almost every Sunday my family attended our Catholic service and then I drove us over to GT. We were learning so much about ourselves, how to please God and actually live for him. Never had Pamela and I experienced such a thirst for God. It made us feel so liberated. Even my children seemed more at home at the new church.

After visiting the church for months, Pamela and I made the decision to leave the Catholic church. It was so hard for me to do. Leaving it was like stabbing my family in the back. My dad was so hard up about being a devout Catholic, and my siblings couldn't understand why I was leaving it. They just didn't know that I felt nothing while sitting in the Catholic services, and yet at GTaustin, I could practically feel God's love saturating me. They didn't get it. Even when I tried to introduce them to my new outlook on Jesus, they rejected me.

One particular afternoon, my brother Eli confided in

me about his marriage problems. He wanted to divorce his wife, but I believed they could work it out. Pamela and I had experienced our own troubles in our relationship, and yet we trusted God to help us. I felt certain God could do the same for my brother and sister-in-law.

"I know you and Jillian are having problems, Eli, but you shouldn't give up on your marriage. All marriages experience issues every now and then; we just have to stick it out. You can't turn your back on her and file for divorce."

"I don't know, Dwayne." Eli shrugged his shoulders and propped his elbows on the table. He rested his forehead in his hand and picked at his dinner. "We're different from when we were younger. We just don't have that love for one another that we once had. That spark, it's not there anymore."

"Don't take this the wrong way, Eli." I eyed him warily. "But, I don't believe God wants you to get a divorce. I think you should turn your life over to God and completely receive Jesus into your heart."

Eli chuckled. "What are you talking about? How could that possibly save my marriage? Don't start with any of that crazy Christian talk to me. I don't want to hear it."

"It's not crazy. Accepting Jesus as the center of your life and placing him at the head of your marriage will save it. I'm telling you, Eli. God can save you and Jillian. He can fix any problem you're facing."

He laughed sharply. "How do you even know there is a God?"

"Aw, c'mon. Don't start that."

"No, I'm serious! The Bible talks about all these marvelous and miraculous things about God, heaven, Jesus and all that. But what about the stuff it doesn't mention? What about the verses that make absolutely no sense whatsoever? Have you even questioned it?"

"No." I shook my head. "And I don't need to. I have faith in God. He's shown himself to me a number of times and proved his existence even when he didn't need to. God —"

"Forget it, Dwayne." Eli scraped his chair against the floor. "I don't know who you think you are now since you've hung up your Catholic faith and become a Christian, but it's really pissing me off. I'm out of here. It was nice seeing you, brother."

I hung my head as stress overcame me. My newfound love for God was causing me to lose my family. Some family members were receptive to my message, but Eli was one I just couldn't get through to. I was so amazed by God and his splendor. I wanted to share my sense of joy and trust in God with the world.

Dad was another one I couldn't talk to about my love for God. So, I started anonymously sending him Christian tracts in the mail. If he wouldn't receive the message of hope in Jesus from me, then hopefully the tracts would touch him. I also prayed for God to send a macho man my father's way. I knew the sort of guys my dad automatically respected. They had to exude respect and manliness, and I knew he'd only listen to a man as strong as himself.

ତ~ତ~ତ~

Years later, in my early 40s, I believed God answered my prayers about my father. My pastor called me and said he had something to tell me.

"Dwayne, you'll never guess what a buddy of mine just told me."

I chuckled at his enthusiasm. "Oh, yeah? What?"

"My pastor friend called me earlier and said he ran into your father in a parking lot. He just started talking to him about Jesus, forgiveness and giving his life over to the Lord. He said your dad was so receptive of his message that he got on his knees and asked God for forgiveness. Right there in the parking lot! Can you believe it?"

"My dad?" I questioned. "My father!?"

"YES!" He laughed. "All those prayers, for all these years. God came through for you."

I stood with the receiver nestled against my shoulder, completely speechless. I believed God would save my father from his mean ways one day, but I was still so amazed at God. After I hung up with my pastor, I thanked God for sending someone for my father to talk to.

Four years later, my father passed away. During his terminal illness, he wasn't the cruel and unbalanced man I'd always known him to be. He was different. I believe God gave my father a chance to undo all his wrongdoings that day in the parking lot. When my dad asked Jesus into his heart, I believe God replaced his stony heart with a much softer one.

Some years ago, I started memorizing scripture. I felt strongly that this was something I should do. Just as David from the Bible tells the Lord, "I have hidden your word in my heart that I might not sin against you" (Psalm 119:11). The more I read, studied and sought to understand God, the stronger I became as a Christian man. Through this practice, God taught me the importance of spending time with him. I didn't only memorize the scriptures for myself — I did it for others. People often came to me and asked for prayer because they were able to see God in me.

I liked being able to listen to their circumstances and quickly state a passage in the Bible that pertained to their situation.

I've learned that the power of God is not in *our* words, but in *his* word. And I believe his word can only be found in the Bible. His word provides strength for the weak, hope for the downtrodden, care for the forgotten ones, confidence for the self-loathing, healing for the wounded and love for the ones like me. The ones who grew up feeling unworthy and unloved.

I started leaving Christ-related tracts everywhere I went, just hoping they would speak a much-needed word into someone's life.

Throughout my life, I always thought I had to behave a certain way to be like all the men in my family before me. Like a generational curse, I fell into the trap of drinking to cope with my issues, taking my wonderful wife for granted, using my career and bankroll to determine my worth and not putting God first in my life. But as the Bible reads, "Create in me a pure heart, O God, and renew a steadfast spirit within me" (Psalm 51:10), the Lord altered my mindset, purified the intentions of my heart and showed me a new way of living. *He changed me.*

I didn't realize that I could *truly* be like the men on my mother's side — good men who possessed a deep love for Jesus. I wanted to, but I thought I was fated to become my father. I didn't know family patterns could be broken, that a man could become something different than what the other men in his family were.

But I suppose God knew that all along.

ON A COLLISION COURSE
The Story of James and Connie
Written by Shelley Jean Lowery

James

I gladly took the cold beverage a young man offered me, thanking him, then popped the top and took a drink. It tasted good.

It was a beautiful day for a family reunion, although I'll admit it felt a little odd to be attending another family's reunion. But Rebecca and her brothers had invited us, and we looked forward to seeing them.

We followed the signs that told us we were in the right place. I looked around for Rebecca and her brothers and turned to ask my wife, Connie, if she saw them.

"Are you James?" I turned to see a man and woman coming up behind us.

"I've looked forward to meeting you!" A tall gentleman in an even taller cowboy hat thrust his hand out for me to shake.

"I'm Tim. Uncle Tim. And this is Nancy, my wife. Rebecca and the boys have been telling us about the accident and what a hero you are."

"Oh, I'm no hero. I did what anyone would have done in the same circumstances."

"Hey, James! Connie! I wondered when you were going to get here!"

I turned to see Rebecca running in our direction with a smile as big as the Texas sky. She nearly knocked me over with a big bear hug, and I gladly accepted her embrace. She hugged Connie with just as much vigor and began to rattle on about how I had saved her life. A crowd of family members began to form, and I was asked to tell the story several times. Rebecca interrupted often, to add her account of what had happened.

"James is my hero!" Rebecca said with a smile.

We later saw the boys, Caleb and Jeremiah, and their parents, Elizabeth and Mark. We were introduced to the entire family, and we spent the day laughing, joking and eating. And, of course, I was asked to tell the story of the day of the accident. I tried to make light of it, but the family wouldn't have any part of that. To all of them, I was a hero.

It was starting to get dark by the time Connie and I said our goodbyes and climbed into our big Dodge truck.

"What a wonderful family. I'm glad we came."

Connie smiled at me as she said it. She then reached over and placed her hand on top of mine as I gripped the shifter and moved it into first gear. I took my time in answering. I felt very emotional. Something I tried to choke back. I didn't like to show my emotions. I grew up believing it was a sign of weakness. Intuitively, I think she knew I was feeling emotionally fragile and was trying to lend her support.

"Yes," I said. "I'm glad we came."

Then I chuckled. "I should have brought a tape player

and just played a recording of what happened the day of the accident! It would have been a lot less work."

"Oh, James! They were just so appreciative for what you did for Rebecca. You really did save her life, and they wanted you to know how grateful they are."

I drove in silence and chewed on the day's events. Thinking it through until we finally drove into our driveway, I shifted into neutral, set the emergency brake and shut off the engine. I then turned in my seat and looked at Connie.

"I feel like Rebecca is somehow saving *my* life."

ở ở ở

Connie

Stretched out before us was a tangle of subdivisions, with every intersection leading to neighborhoods. Neighborhoods with homes and homes with families. Families with children sleeping. I glanced back to the car seat where our son slept. The hum of the car always put him to sleep. I turned back around and stared out the passenger-side window.

"I wish there were two car seats," I mumbled to myself, and as I did, I caught a glimpse of my reflection that bounced back off of the cold glass window. The deep sadness was apparent, and I frowned at myself.

Winding through the neighborhood, I watched the houses pass as James and I made our way to the highway. It was odd for me to think of those sleeping inside the homes we passed. The homes looked so nice and neat. So "Hallmark" perfect at night. But if those walls could talk, what stories would they tell?

I wonder if there are women in those houses who cry themselves to sleep at night?

I stared in silence and imagined their agony was the same as mine.

"Oh, honey," James would tell me. "Don't worry. You can try to have another baby."

Others would say, "There will be another chance to have a baby. Besides, you have a beautiful little boy. Be thankful for him."

The words would cut like a knife every time I heard them. Friends, neighbors and even family members would try to console me with those awful words.

"Don't you get it!" I wanted to scream at them after each miscarriage. "My baby just died!"

౼౼౼

Mom always said I wouldn't amount to anything. My very first memory was around age 2 or 3. I remember Mom choking me and screaming, "I wish you had never been born!" The sting of her words always hurt far worse than her fist, although the beatings were pretty bad.

Dad served in the Navy, and we only saw him a couple of months out of the year. The rest of the time, the five of us kids were Mom's responsibility. And most of the time, well, she couldn't handle it. I hated when she would beat my brothers and sisters. It made me despise her. When I was 9, she nearly killed my 5-year-old sister by beating her head against the wooden floor. While she lay in a coma for four days with a skull fracture, I told myself I would *never* be like her. I would be a good mother and love and nurture my children.

But many years and four miscarriages later, I started to really believe I was a failure. I was broken. The doctor said so. He said I probably had bad eggs. *Bastard!* I couldn't even be a good woman and have a baby.

Perhaps I'm being punished, I thought. *Maybe God knows I would be a bad mother so he won't allow me to have more children.*

ࡣࡣࡣ

The interstate stretched before us on our long journey to Tennessee. Our headlights cast a ghostlike glow across the road. There was a solace in traveling at night. Everything looked pristine. The daylight is exposing. Light reveals the reality of things. I preferred some things hidden in the cloak of night's darkness, like a blanket draped over the cares of the day. I wished it was that easy. To just turn off the light and not face the ugly pain of my childhood beatings or my barrenness.

ࡣࡣࡣ

James

My head pounded, and I worked to open my eyes. I heard the sounds around me but wished I couldn't because they made my head want to explode.

I thought to myself, *Shit! What did I do last night?* I was hung over and trying desperately to remember what had happened at the Marine Corps Ball the night before. I struggled to my feet, and guilt washed over me.

I had been sober for three years, with the help of Alcoholics Anonymous, before being sent to Japan with the Marine Corps. Japan was a nice enough place. Probably the politest nation in the world. I think the Japanese intuitively understood that politeness was the lubricant that made the gears of a society turn smoothly. But I was not feeling polite. I wanted to cuss. Or throw something. Or both.

"I cannot start drinking again!" I told myself. "I will die a miserable death like my stepfather if I don't get help!"

My dad was a hardworking man. But taking care of my mother and working late hours left me and my brother at the mercy of my mother. My mother had been diagnosed as schizophrenic, and she lived in a state of rage most of the time. When she consistently took her medication, it kept her symptoms at bay, but for years she went untreated, and the results were horrific. Growing up with an un-medicated paranoid schizophrenic mother wasn't pretty. Her emotional disconnection from her acts. Her deterioration into an unkempt, almost beastlike state. It's a lot for a little boy to understand, and Dad was never around much to comfort us boys. When Mom went into a mental hospital, I actually exhaled for the first time in years. Imagine my surprise when two days later, she came home. Drugged up on Thorazine.

Dad was a type 1 diabetic, and when I was 15, he died from an insulin reaction. As the oldest child, I felt the responsibility to keep the family together, but I dealt with my grief by acting out at school, bullying my peers and trying to control something — anything — in my out-of-control life. I sniffed glue, skipped school and eventually dropped out nearly one year after Dad's passing.

Mom remarried, to an alcoholic. He was a verbally abusive man, and he nearly drank us out of house and home. He did manage to keep my brother Chuck and me out of serious trouble, and he taught us right from wrong, although he did not practice it much. He put me to work cutting and selling firewood and doing other odd jobs. He also taught me how to drink — a habit I would battle in the years to come. His alcoholic ways ended their marriage only one year after it started.

Mom kicked him out, and he left, leaving us flat broke.

࿐࿐࿐

Uncle Ronnie sat on the living room sofa drinking a cold glass of lemonade that Mom had poured for him. She retreated to the kitchen to talk with Aunt Sue. Ronnie leaned forward and placed his elbows on his knees and locked eyes with mine.

"How are you getting along, young man?"

I mumbled at him, "I'm doing all right, I guess." It wasn't a very convincing reply.

"Why don't you come work for me, James? I'll give you a job and teach you the carpentry trade."

We agreed that I would work for him at the shop. Uncle Ronnie was a good man, and he treated me well, but the business was in decline. Times were hard, and we weren't getting enough work. So after a disagreement with my uncle, I marched down to the Marine Corps office and enlisted. I was 20 years old.

କିକିକି

Connie

I thought to myself, *I must be crazy! What if he's a jerk, and I'm stuck with him all day?*

I glanced down at my watch and checked myself in the mirror as I heard James pull into my driveway. I ran across the living room to the window, and as I pulled back the curtain, I could feel my pulse rise. I was anxious to get a look at him.

When James stepped out of his truck, I was pleasantly surprised by his good looks, and I secretly hoped he would feel the same about me.

He's in great shape. Of course he is! He's in the Marine Corps.

The doorbell rang. I took a long, deep breath and opened the door.

"Hi. You must be James?"

I blushed.

We rode together to Knott's Berry Farm, and we labored to keep a conversation going. I was relieved when we pulled into the parking lot of the amusement park and James turned off the engine. We walked together across the parking lot. It wasn't the best day to spend at the park. The weather report called for rain. But this was what we had arranged. My best friend, Lisa, had set me up on this blind date, and I wasn't going to "chicken out" and hear her ranting about it all day.

We decided to catch a few rides before we ate, and it was a good thing we did because we only got to ride a couple of roller coasters before it started to rain. We were both painfully shy and didn't say much the first hour or so. But as we grew more comfortable, we spent a lot of our day talking. James was pleasant to be around, and I was so delighted by the end of the night that I kissed him, and he told me he would like to see me again.

I smiled and said, "Yes, I would like that."

We didn't get to see each other as much as I would have liked. James was sent to Yuma, Arizona, with the Marine Corps only two months after we met. We spent as much time together as we could. A day or two, a couple of times a month, when James could get leave. Between visits, we wrote letters nearly every day. We were married a year later. I was 20 years old. James was 22.

Married life was wonderful at first, but then the fighting began. I was smoking cigarettes and pot and drinking as well. It was a way of escape, I think. Numbing the pain in my heart. I longed to be happy and thought that getting married and getting away from my dysfunctional family would bring me happiness, but it seems I brought the dysfunction with me.

It turned out that James was an alcoholic. I felt trapped. Alcoholism ran rampant on both sides of my family. I was angry at the world and miserable to be around. It was when I became pregnant that I decided to stop drinking and smoking. One of us needed to be sober to raise our son, and it wasn't going to be James.

Perhaps I'll find happiness when I have a baby.

My father was a career Navy man, and our family moved a lot. We moved five times before my 5th birthday, and by the time I was 9, we were living in Japan. My parents' marriage was like two alley cats tied together at the tail and thrown over a clothesline — they were together, but there was no unity. They fought constantly, except when they went days without talking to each other. My mother hated me, and she made that very clear in what she said and did to me.

I think happiness is 100 percent relational: Our relationships with other people are more important than we think. My unhappiness was completely intertwined with other people — family, friends and neighbors. Every one of my relationships was broken, and I had moved from place to place my entire life. I always looked for happiness at the next location. I was in a misery loop. My unhappiness was a breeding ground for mistrust, which brought on more unhappiness, which led to more mistrust. I hated everyone around me. But, most of all, I hated myself.

ॐॐॐ

James

It had been a long day at work, and I looked forward to going home and relaxing. Stepping inside, I looked around for Connie and then walked down the hall to our bedroom. As I drew closer, I could hear Connie crying. *Oh, great,* I thought. Standing in the doorway, I asked why she was crying.

"Why do you think?" she snapped back at me. "I had another miscarriage."

"Oh," I said. "What happened this time?"

"What's it matter?" she cried. "It's always my fault."

Sadness rushed through me every time Connie had a miscarriage. This would have been her eighth miscarriage. Or perhaps her ninth? I didn't know what to say to comfort her, so, as usual, I plopped down in my chair and turned on the television. And tried to focus on something else. Anything else.

Connie went through a terrible succession of emotions with each miscarriage. And I dreaded the outburst of anger that would raise its ugly head. It became a more regular occurrence for me as well, and with every miscarriage, our fighting escalated. I often came home to find Connie crying. It was the first sign that she was sinking into depression again.

I tried to hide my own sadness. I, too, was struggling and wondered if I should just end it all. I tried to feel better. But it seemed the cycle continued, no matter what I tried. I felt out of control. I just couldn't make myself happy, nor could I make Connie happy.

❧❧❧

Connie

I would often lie in bed and stare up at the ceiling fan. I didn't want to get out of bed and face the day. What was the point? I felt like such a failure. I had been a disappointment to my mother and to my husband and children. I wished I could just fall asleep and never wake up.

Life would be so much better for everyone, I would think to myself. *James would have a better life if I wasn't here.*

As I headed to the kitchen one morning, I replayed my fight with James the night before. I opened the refrigerator and stood and stared at its contents. I hadn't been grocery shopping in days. In fact, the entire house was a mess. I just couldn't muster the strength to clean it. This was often the case when I got depressed. I could not seem to accomplish the simplest of tasks. I didn't want to do anything but go bury myself in bed and pull the covers over my head. But instead, I forced myself to grab my purse and car keys from the kitchen counter and head out the door.

I started the engine on the Buick and put it into reverse. *I guess I'll go to the grocery store,* I thought. With my head still swimming with dark thoughts, I wanted to just end it all.

Then I saw it — the freeway bridge ahead.

I could drive my car off of the bridge and end all of this. I'm sure it would be a relief to James. He wouldn't have to deal with me anymore and could just go on with his life and find happiness.

I drove toward the bridge. It was the first time in days I had made up my mind about anything. *It's settled.*

But as I drove in the direction of the bridge, I heard a gentle voice whisper to me, *Please don't do this! I can fix it! My precious child, I love you!*

That gentle voice persuaded me to change my decision to end my life in that moment. I drove to the grocery store parking lot, turned off the engine and sat in the car and sobbed.

ҩҩҩ

James

I cannot say I'd been an ideal member of AA, but I had pretty much stayed sober. Connie had lost nine out of 11 pregnancies, but we had successfully given birth to a baby boy and then a girl. After our daughter was born, we decided that I should have a vasectomy. Things seemed to be going pretty good at home. We were trying to be happy.

It was on a Sunday in May that I received a phone call telling me that Mom had gone off her meds and was out of control. I took leave from work and had her committed to the state mental hospital. It was one of the hardest things I ever had to do. I knew it's what needed to happen — I was giving her an opportunity to heal or at least get the treatment she needed. She didn't want to be committed, and she cussed me all the way to the hospital.

The mental hospital is not a place I wanted to be placing my mother. They locked her in, and she was not allowed to voluntarily leave. Only family members could visit. Everything was taken from her that she could hurt herself with. It was not a fun place to be. I felt very alone the day I had to commit Mom. I cried outwardly as I drove home. One year later, Mom passed away.

I had struggled with depression before, but things seemed to worsen after Mom's passing. I began to question my own sanity. It really scared me. I thought perhaps I was going nuts, just like Mom.

What if I'm crazy, too? My thoughts became darker, and I thought, too often, about taking my life. There came a point when I could no longer ensure my safety or the safety of my family. I had myself committed to the same mental hospital where I'd placed my mother. I stayed a few days, saw a doctor and he put me on "happy pills." They helped me stabilize. I could breathe easier, and the darkness began to lift.

I soon retired from the Marine Corps and moved my family to Austin, Texas. I began working for a good company and settled down. I didn't go much to Alcoholics Anonymous anymore but stayed sober by staying busy with home and work projects.

I was working on a Sunday afternoon and trying to get between jobs quickly. I finished up on the first job and headed toward the second. I was about halfway there when my phone rang, and I was asked to return to the first job. Normally, I wouldn't go straight back to a job that I had just left, but I swung the truck around and headed back. Retracing my route, I rounded the corner. As I did, I noticed a commotion in the road. I slowed and noticed a head-on collision between a minivan and a Suburban.

The accident must have just taken place because I had passed that exact spot only minutes prior. The scene of the accident was directly across from a church, and people from the congregation were already assisting. I noticed one of the passengers was stepping out of the minivan. I thought everything was under control, and I started to pass around the wreck. Looking back, I noticed that the passenger who had stepped out of the vehicle was still in the same spot. The other passenger was a young girl, and she was stuck in her seatbelt, which was holding her in place.

I immediately pulled over and said a quick prayer, "God help us!" Then I jumped out of my truck. I did a quick assessment of the scene and found out how everyone was faring. The two boys in the front seat were conscious with some minor injuries. Caleb, the driver, said he was okay. Jeremiah, the front passenger, was asking what had happened. He had been knocked silly by the airbag. The driver of the Suburban was conscious and being assisted by another woman. The front doors were stuck shut, and I told the boys they would have to wait a little bit.

The young girl who was stuck in her seatbelt was pretty hysterical, and a woman was doing her best to keep her calm. I asked the woman, "What's your name?"

"Nicole," she said. "And this is Rebecca."

I turned and looked at the young girl and said, "You're going to be all right, honey. We're going to get you out of this seatbelt."

My adrenaline was pumping at this point, and my Marine Corps training kicked into high gear. I was glad Nicole was there — she was far braver than I was. Everything in me wanted to run away, but Nicole's presence steadied me. I told Nicole to hold tightly to Rebecca because I was going to cut her out of the seatbelt that held her in place. Once the belt was cut, Rebecca dropped into Nicole's arms, and I went to my truck to look for a tarp for the ground and tools to work on the doors. Although there did not appear to be any imminent danger to the boys in the front of the van, I was determined to get the doors open.

After going through the bins in my truck to find tools to work on the doors, I heard a voice say to me, *What are you doing? She needs you!* I looked around, but there was no one standing near me. The voice had been crisp and clear. There was no doubt what I had heard, and there was no time to assess its source. I went right back to Rebecca as the voice had told me to do.

Nicole and I carried Rebecca to a ditch. I squatted down and placed her legs over my lap. Nicole did her best to calm Rebecca down. She was scared. So was I. I had first aid training while in the Marine Corps, but I never had to use it to this degree. Outwardly, Rebecca looked like she would be fine, but then the bruises started to show up across her neck and lower abdomen. This worried me, and I knew she probably had some internal injuries.

"God, help me!" I prayed out of fear. "What should I do?"

And, as simply as I had asked, I felt like God answered, *Just hold her still.*

I didn't move. It took some time for the ambulance to arrive, but I stayed there, just holding Rebecca still until they arrived and braced her on a board for transport. I took a few photos of the accident scene with my phone. I'm not sure why I thought to do so, but I did. I talked to Nicole before leaving and thanked her for her help.

Then I walked over to a nearby fence and fell apart.

Before long, I was surrounded by folks from the church who prayed over me, filling me with strength. Then I got into my work truck and tried to resume my day's duties.

Adrenaline still surged through me like volts of electricity. When I arrived at my next job, I just sat in the vehicle for a while and tried to calm myself. After about 30 minutes, I decided I was okay, and I went to work but couldn't get my mind to stay on task. That night I relayed the day's events to Connie, and it seemed to help just talking about it.

I was working at a job three days later when I received a call from a manager of another crew. He asked me what had happened that Sunday, and I had to pull off the road to relate the abbreviated version of the accident. He then told me the family was trying to find out who had saved their daughter's life. I had been an emotional wreck since the accident, and this just sent me over. I tried not to cry, but I couldn't help myself. I was just so grateful. I hadn't told anyone about the voice I had heard that day. The voice that had told me to go back and help Rebecca. I believed it had to have been God.

The manager told me that Rebecca had internal perforations and a torn aorta. The aorta could have ruptured if she had been allowed to move or walk around. I had done as the voice had told me. I didn't know Rebecca's internal injuries, but I concluded God surely did.

I found the circumstances of that day to be constantly on my mind. I felt emotional at times for no reason. It was like my insides had been tenderized. I went to the hospital trying to find Rebecca, but I had the wrong last name. I went again with the right name, and they had just checked her out of the hospital.

Perhaps I'm not supposed to meet them, I thought. Only weeks later, I received a call from Rebecca's parents, and we arranged to meet at the park. We felt an instant connection with them. The following summer, we were invited to their family reunion.

We were grateful to see the kids doing so well and to feel the outpouring of love that this family offered us. We also learned more about their family and the troubling times they had made it through by relying on their faith in God. Several people at the reunion invited us to go to church with them at GTaustin. It appeared that most of those attending the family celebration went to church there. Normally I would have blown off an invitation to go to church, but there was something tangibly different about this family. Something I couldn't just dismiss.

There was an optimism and happiness that permeated their lives. A deep joy and peace that I think I had longed for my entire life. Connie and I said our goodbyes to the family and got into the truck. I put the key in the ignition, but before turning it on, I sat back in my seat and told Connie, "I want what that family has. If I went through the things that they have gone through these last couple of years, I would be a very bitter man."

❧❧❧

Connie

That next Sunday morning, James and I got up and got ready to go to GTaustin. We had decided after the family reunion the week before that we would attend the next church service. It seemed like a good idea at the time, but I was reluctant to go that morning. It had been a long time since I had been to church, and I dreaded that the service might be long, boring and lethargic. But worse than that, I hated the judgmental feelings I got from some church folks. Like I was some kind of terrible sinner. I must admit that Rebecca's family didn't make me feel that way, but I was still nervous.

Attending that Sunday, I was surprised that I felt no judgment. I sensed only love and acceptance, in a way that I never had before. Rebecca's family introduced us to all their friends, and people were genuinely happy to meet us. It wasn't like church I remembered as a child. This place was lively and fun. People ate donuts and drank coffee. They talked and laughed, and then when the music started, I was again pleasantly surprised. It was upbeat and contemporary. No organ music or hymnals in sight. *Hmmm,* I thought to myself. *If this is what church has become, it might just be okay.*

I still had my secret fears. I thought that after they really got to know me, I would be a disappointment. I always had been.

৵৵৵

James

We attended every Sunday after that. We didn't want to miss anything, and we loved seeing our new friends at GTaustin. I noticed changes in Connie. She was different. Her anger was disappearing, and I noticed a joy and kindness taking its place. Connie told me that I was changing, also.

We were learning that God loved us and that we had been on a journey our whole lives to come to that understanding. It was on a Sunday morning when Connie was telling about her journey that I realized it. Plain as day. I had been depressed and suicidal. And so had Connie. God had been drawing us individually, and as a couple, toward himself the entire time. We came to believe in Jesus Christ as our Lord and Savior, and we were both baptized.

The church people told me that they saw the transformation in our lives and our marriage. Our emotional scars were being healed, and we were realizing that nothing was too broken for God to fix.

One Sunday morning, Connie had a severe asthma attack while in church. She used her inhaler, but it wasn't helping. During the service, one of the worship leaders came down from the stage and asked what she could do to help. She placed her hands on Connie's shoulders, and she prayed, asking Jesus to heal her. Connie's breathing began to ease. Connie said it felt like electric shocks all over her ribcage, and she felt sure she was being healed. Since that day, she has no longer needed asthma medicine to breathe.

૱૱૱

We'd been on a collision course for years: Alcohol, fighting, depression, dark suicidal thoughts and layer upon layer of emotional scaring had us living out-of-control lives. But everything changed the day I came upon the accident. And every time I saw Rebecca at church, I was reminded of the day of the car accident. Nothing has been the same since then. It's as though our lives collided with the God who created us.

We became different. Where once there was anger, that was replaced with a deep sense of peace and joy. Where loneliness permeated our lives, we built deep and lasting friendships. Where physical sickness tormented us for years, we enjoy healthy bodies. And where depression once drove us to suicidal thoughts of wanting to end our lives, we became filled with hopefulness for the future.

LOVED
The Story of Kayla
Written by Arlene Showalter

"Just take one step at a time." I put one foot on a riser and hoisted my body forward. "Now another."

I inched myself up the stairwell, which felt like a dark tunnel of doom. My chosen destiny awaited me at the top.

"Only a few more, and it's all over, Kayla." I continued coaching myself until I reached the upper landing and moved toward my bedroom. "Just a few more."

I sank onto my empty king bed. My shoulders sagged. I cried no tears. I felt no sorrow. *I am the walking dead.*

I emptied every bottle of prescription medications onto my bedspread and downed them all with what was left of my bottle of wine. *Ah, my little saviors. You are my ticket out of this hell.*

❧❧❧

"Da's home." My mammy (mother) stopped mid-note as we both heard the key turn in the door. "We'll finish the song later," she whispered and slipped me a few coins. I scampered off to my bedroom and closed the door with a silent click just as the front door slapped open.

"Dublin's filled with eejitts (idiots)," Daddy roared as he stamped into the house. I heard him plop himself in his favorite chair. "Mindless, stupid eejitts."

"Why is that, Kane?" Ma kept her voice light and pleasant.

"They're all yapping about some stupid show on the telly. Really, only brainless people watch that goggle box. We'll not have one in this house."

"I know how much you hate the television, Kane. Come along while your dinner is hot."

The moment I heard him move to the kitchen, I wafted out the front door. Ma's coins jingled in my pocket. She knew I hated to be around Da's rants of how our society was headed to hell in a handbag. I used the money to purchase candy from our local grocery and ate without his strident voice ringing in my ears.

I was the youngest of six children. Me mammy's energy dissipated with each birth, and by the time I arrived, she was worn out. Unaware of her condition, this high-energy child bounced into life, ready to take on the world.

She spoiled me and sheltered me from Da's melancholy rants, while my older siblings expressed their resentment.

"She's so irresponsible."

"She'll grow up to be of no use, Mammy."

"You need to discipline her more."

"She's a bad child."

"She's nothing but a guttersnipe," they said, calling me the Irish equivalent of "white trash."

I ran the streets to stay away from my father, and Mammy financed my forays into the neighborhood. When

I realized the good kids in our area went to bed earlier than I wished to go home, I explored the neighborhood beyond ours. Wild kids stayed out as late as they pleased. I fancied that and eagerly joined their capers.

৵৵৵

In the late 1970s, every Irish school had a disco, as did our local school. Older kids snuck alcohol to the playground area and imbibed before going inside to dance.

"Have a drink, Kayla."

"Sure. Thanks." Never one to shy away from new adventures, I reached for the proffered bottle and drank deeply. As the liquid slid down my throat, I felt comforting warmth, and it washed away all my shyness, especially around boys.

The new emboldened me marched into the dance hall, full of courage and wit. Later, I took a break from dancing to visit the ladies room.

This is great, I thought as I sat on the toilet. The graffiti-splashed walls of the stall spun around me. *The guys are asking me to dance. People are laughing at my jokes. I feel fantastic!*

By 13, I'd mastered the tandem skills of drinking while dancing. Alcohol became my new best friend, and I quickly learned not to do *anything* without it. It drowned out my growing feelings of worthlessness cultivated by my siblings and further distanced me from the "good" kids in my neighborhood. And it helped catapult me into life's next adventure.

"Check this out." Colin, a boy I'd met hanging around a fish n' chips shop, held something out for me to see.

"What is it?"

"Marijuana. You afraid to try it?"

"I'm not afraid of anything. Let me have some."

LSD followed pot. Never once did a flicker of fear or common sense pass through my thoughts.

"The best of luck to ye," I told Colin as he left for London with our friend Dickie. "I hope you find work soon."

My phone rang some six hours later. "Hello, Dickie. What's up?"

"He's dead." Dickie's voice came thick and heavy over the wire.

"Who?" An uneasy feeling settled in my stomach.

"Colin."

"*Colin?*" My voice rose to an agonized shriek. "How? When? Why?" My mind spun out of control.

"At a loo in London. He overdosed."

I stumbled to my room and threw myself across my bed, idly tracing the squiggly red lines up my arms. My strongest link to Colin. My fingers stilled. *It could have been me. I could be dead at 18, but I'm not. I'm alive, and Colin is dead.*

I swore off heroin and downed alcohol even more to soothe and satisfy the growing emptiness in my heart.

෨෨෨

"How romantic," I sighed a few months later while watching the British film *Not Quite Paradise*, a story of six Brits and Americans who volunteer at a kibbutz (meaning communal living) in Israel. The plot revolved around a romance between an Israeli girl and an American boy. "Wouldn't it be fun to find love in a kibbutz?"

I talked my dad into letting me go, assuring him that the experience would build character, a quality he surely wished for me, a high school dropout going no place fast. With my usual "act now and ponder later" attitude, I packed my haversack with Ireland's tricolor flag of green, white and orange splashed across its flap.

I tucked a few bottles of good Irish whiskey and rolling papers inside my sack for selling, but on my first night in an Israeli hostel, I broke one out and helped myself and everyone around me get hammered. I also carried thousands of dollars in counterfeit money, which I exchanged on the black market. After my money — real and fake — ran out, I joined the realm of the homeless.

I met up with two other girls, Hadda from Iceland and Aggie from England. We decided to travel to the kibbutz near Galilee together.

They tossed us out.

"We are not a hotel. Our work is serious here."

"Holy-moley. What's the harm of having a little fun

here and there?" I complained to my equally inebriated companions.

We moved on to another kibbutz and eventually wore out our welcome there, so we took to crashing in the town square with other displaced/homeless/rootless people.

"Why are you girls staying here in the square?" a stocky stranger asked as I was panhandling. "Do you not know this isn't safe?"

"No place to go." I shrugged. "No money, either."

"My name is Ivan. Please, I want to help you."

"How?"

"I will find you a place. You cannot stay here."

Ivan put me up in his house. He contacted a couple with a baby, and they hired me as a nanny. They also gave me a room to live in.

"Kayla, your brother-in-law is on the phone," my employer told me. "Interpol has been trying to find you for weeks. He says it's an emergency."

I picked up the phone.

"Hello?"

"Hi, Davin. This is Kayla. What do you want?"

"Kayla. We've been trying to get in touch with you." The familiar impatient tone crept across the wire. "Your da died weeks ago. We couldn't hold the funeral because we couldn't find you." The tone turned accusatory. "Your ma needs you. You need to get home — now."

I headed to the local liquor store and purchased several bottles of vodka. Once back in my room, I shut the door and began guzzling, as hard and fast as possible.

"Kayla." Ivan's light tap sounded on the door. "Please open the door."

"Go away," I cried. "Leave me alone."

"Please, Kayla. This is not a good time to be alone. Please open the door."

"Go away. Go away." *I don't deserve any kind words right now. How could I fail my mammy so?*

I heard footsteps recede. I drank until a blackout freed my mind.

৵৵৵

"I'll have another shot," I told the barkeep as my gaze wandered beyond the dirty pub window. Across the lane, stone and wooden crosses marched, some tipped and tipsy, like me, but from age. *I can't go face his grave yet.*

I drank until my legs threatened to give out. Then, I tottered out the door and over to the graveyard, looking for the freshest mound of dirt. Once there, I threw myself down and wept.

"Da, Da, I'm so sorry. Sorry I wasn't here when you died. Sorry I wasn't the daughter you wanted and gave you so much trouble. Sorry I wasn't as smart as you. Sorry I quit high school. I promise you that though I'm 17, I'll go back and get my diploma. I'll make you proud of me someday, Da. I promise that someday I'll be good enough for your love. I'm sorry I have failed you and the family so badly. I'm so, so sorry."

Saying sorry didn't bring relief to my broken heart, no matter how many times I said it.

I settled in with Ma, who hated living alone, and went on the public dole due to massive unemployment in Ireland in the 1980s. She allowed me to bring any friends I wanted into the house to drink and play board games. Da never allowed guests, so while I rejoiced in my new freedom, guilt nagged at me for my absence at his death.

☙☙☙

"I have to get out of here," I confided in my friend Maeve. "I'm suffocating."

"How?"

"My siblings go on and on about what a loser I am because I quit high school. They say I'll never amount to anything in life and insist I'll end up canning peas or collecting trash for a living. They treat me like a gurrier, and I can't take it anymore." Yet another word for "white trash."

"So, what do you fancy doing?"

"Let's go to the Continent. We'll have a whale of a time!"

"Jolly good. Count me in."

We took off and found jobs as chambermaids in Munich. Maeve and I continued our practice of drinking way too much — especially Maeve. After working and saving our money for 18 months, we decided to go "on the road," a popular European phrase meaning to wander around the continent, drinking and getting high.

Maeve and I embraced our new adventure, traveling

through different countries by day and drinking ourselves into oblivion at night. Our money ran out on the French Riviera, so we found more jobs to finance the next leg of our ramblings.

When Maeve and I returned to Ireland, I missed Europe and longed for the distance it provided between my siblings and me. I went back and began hitchhiking all over Italy.

One day a doctor picked me up. His name was Angelo. He knew a smidgeon of English and I, a pinch of Italian. We hit it off right away, but I knew he fancied me when I heard him tell a friend that I had *bella occhi* (beautiful eyes). We became a couple, and I followed him to Sicily to visit his mother. There, we gathered with a large group of friends on the beach one night.

"Ciao, Angelo! Ciao, Kayla!" The guys raised their glasses in greeting.

"*Sláinte.*"

I held my own bottle aloft. "Cheers."

"Kayla, why is it every time I see you, you have a beer in your hand?" Nico asked with a gentle smile.

"Isn't everyone drinking here?"

"Yes, but not beer."

I looked around. Bottles of Sprite, Coca Cola and other soft drinks. Not one other person held a beer.

"I'm Irish," I said, laughing. "You can't be Irish and *not* drink."

Later, the young people began dancing. I remembered my prowess to drink and dance, honed in my early teens.

None of the dancers reached for an alcoholic beverage. I felt heavy — empty.

"I want to take a walk on the beach," I whispered in Angelo's ear.

"I come with you?"

"No, you stay here with your friends. I just want to enjoy hearing the ocean and a little quiet."

"Ciao. I'll be waiting for you."

The endless waves reached for me and receded. Reaching. Receding. Reaching. Receding. I felt pulled like the tide and pushed like the waves. Pulled into the taunts of my siblings while longing and pushing to make something of my life.

"Kayla, why do you always have a beer in your hand?" Nico's words echoed in my mind.

God, do I really have a problem? Why am I so flawed? Is my drinking out of control? I want to be like these people. They seem so happy, and not one is drinking anything harder than Coke.

"I need to go home," I told Angelo. "I have to get my life together once and for all. I never expected to live to 30, but I need to get educated, just in case."

"I am sorry to see you go, but I understand."

I moved in with Ma again and enrolled in school to complete my high school education.

৵৵৵

"Blessed Mary." I dared not pray to God or Jesus. I wasn't anywhere near good enough for that. Tears soaked my cheeks and blouse as I knelt in our family church where Da and I attended Mass. "Am I worthless? Is there no hope for me? I'm almost 29. My first love died from an overdose. I had to leave Angelo in Italy. Can you please, please put someone in my life who will love me as I am and not just for sex? I have so much love to give. I need to find a decent man."

"Kayla, let's go out on Thursday to celebrate your birthday," my friend Karan said.

"You know I never go out on a weeknight. I have to study for school." I had graduated high school and was taking a travel course because I wanted to open my own travel agency.

"It's your birthday."

"I know. I'll celebrate on Saturday."

"It's not the same. Your birthday comes only once a year. You can bend your own rule for one day. Please!"

"Okay, I'll go."

I met Karan at the local pub, never bothering to get dressed up. No makeup or done hair for me. I had more important things on my mind.

I plopped down on a stool next to a stranger. He smiled.

"Hi, I'm Andrew. From the United States."

I took in his brown eyes and hair and tossed my own.

"Kayla, from Dublin. What're you doing here?"

"Business. My company's building a factory right outside your city."

Andrew joined my birthday celebration, and I found him easy to talk to.

"It's midnight!" Karan cried.

"Have to kiss you." I turned to Andrew. "It's Irish tradition."

"I think I could get used to that." He grinned, and our lips touched.

"Would you like to come up to my room?" he asked later.

My eyebrows arched.

"For a cup of tea," he said.

"For tea? Maybe." Then my eyes narrowed. "Are you married? I don't mess around with married men."

"Yes — and no." Andrew sighed. "I left my wife a while back. She's determined to drain me of every cent, so I'm embroiled in a messy divorce."

"What happened?"

"We were never a fit. I tried to stay because we have two children, but I finally concluded that watching their parents' incessant fighting was worse than my leaving." His eyes turned to brown pools of sorrow. "I feel so guilty, though. They deserve better than this. What is worse, anyway? Bickering parents or an absent father?"

We talked into the wee hours. Afterward, Andrew walked me to the taxi.

"Want to go to a music festival next Saturday?" I asked as I climbed in the backseat.

"Not really."

"Irish music. You can't stay in Ireland and not experience it."

"All right."

Andrew and I clicked from that moment. I moved into his apartment, and we became inseparable. I had found the perfect man. He drank as much as I did — and even *more.*

"I'm leaving for the States next week," Andrew said some four months later.

"I don't even want to think about it."

Within two months, I was on an airplane to join him — permanently.

We couldn't marry because Andrew was still tied up in the bitter divorce proceedings.

We partied away the weekends. I, because that's what I did, and Andrew, to wash away the guilt he felt over leaving his two children.

"We were so unhappy for years," he repeated. "I hung on as long as I could, but finally I came to the conclusion leaving was better than constant fighting." He sighed. "Doesn't make it any easier to fight the fact that I abandoned them. She could drag this divorce on for years."

"I don't care. I'll take you any way I can get you. We were meant to be together."

Andrew's job took him all over the world and for many months at a time. I always went with him. We'd settle into an expatriate community and make friends. I filled my hours teaching the locals English.

Andrew's drinking increased as he wheeled and sealed deals. In most of the host countries, a visit to their bars for social drinking was an acceptable way to relax after conducting business.

After each return to the States, we limited our drinking to Friday and Saturday nights. Then we felt the pressing need to celebrate Sunday football. Then Monday night football. Eventually, we drank every night at our favorite bar.

෨෨෨

"I have to go back to Asia," Andrew told me. After finally getting his divorce, we'd married three years earlier. I'd been attending cosmetology school in Arizona, where we lived.

"You'll have to go without me this time." I clung to him. "I will miss you beyond words."

The light of life dimmed with his departure. I felt more and more depressed, even after securing a job at a salon.

"You want to have a good time?" my co-worker Alicia asked.

"Sure. My life sucks since Andrew left."

"No, I mean a *really* good time." Alicia led me to the back of the salon and handed me a small bag of white powder. We snorted the cocaine together, and my loneliness evaporated. Crack soon followed.

"Ma'am, may I see your driver's license and vehicle registration please?" The tall Arizona trooper bent over until his face came level with mine. "Your driving was very erratic, and I can smell alcohol on your person." He straightened up. "Please step out of the vehicle."

I staggered out.

"I need you to walk heel-to-toe on this white line."

I lurched sideways.

"Sorry, ma'am, but I have to arrest you for DUI. Hands behind your back please."

A month in Arizona's Tent City Jail sobered me up — for a while. Andrew's return helped, too.

∂∾∂∾∂∾

"What are you doing?" Andrew padded into the living room and yawned. He squinted at the clock. "Good lord, Kayla, it's 2 a.m. What's so important that you have to do it now?"

"I'm sorting the CDs."

"It can't wait until morning?"

"Not tired." I returned to my sorting.

"Why are you so wide-awake at this hour?"

I looked directly at him. "Because I'm on coke."

"Promise me you'll stop using."

"I promise."

I wanted to honor my promise, but I couldn't. The dishonesty drove a huge wedge between us. Andrew often searched for and found drugs in my handbag, further eroding any trust in me or my promises.

Hoping a change in geography and friends would help change our lives, we moved to Austin, Texas, but continued drifting further and further apart. Drinking remained the only common ground of our marriage.

Sometime later, I had surgery on my knee. Afterward, I discovered the wonder of painkillers. I could function without the hangover of drink or the aftereffects of cocaine. Plus, they were *legal*.

I began swallowing them by the handful and soon resorted to the *illegal* activity of going from doctor to doctor to meet my growing need.

Andrew couldn't handle having drugs in our lives and moved out of our home. He began meeting other women while out socializing, but alcohol controlled his life like drugs did mine, and he failed to form any lasting relationship.

తతత

"Kayla, our brother died." I received the horrid news shortly after Andrew moved out.

"No, NO! What happened?" I knew he drank heavily.

"He had a heart attack and hit his head on a table when he fell."

"I'm coming home for the funeral."

I moved in with my sister. She laid into me as usual, despite the fact that we had buried my brother the day before. "Why do you think Andrew left? What did you do now to make him leave?"

Like I always do, I ran from everyone.

"Suit yourself," my siblings told me. "You're still a gurrier to the lot of us."

I fled her house in the middle of December and moved into a tiny freezing flat that a friend wasn't using — a flat with no central heat. My husband had left. My brother was dead. I wasn't welcome in my mother's house. I wasn't welcome anywhere. It was the worst of times for me. No one asked me how I was feeling, and all I heard was criticism. The pain was unbearable. I started drinking like never before.

It was just me and the booze, yet again. My only friend.

I developed pneumonia and spent a miserable Christmas alone. I called Andrew in desperation. He got me a flight, and I tried to detox in order to get on the plane.

I returned to my house in the United States, feeling like I belonged nowhere. Not Ireland. Not Texas. Cocaine, booze, painkillers. All failed to quash the pain of my vacant heart.

I'm done with it all. Nobody wants me. Maybe I am just a loser like my sisters and brothers insist. Maybe I really am the bad child they say I am. I'll bet not one tear will fall when I end it all.

I gathered all my prescription meds along with a bottle of wine and inched my way upstairs. *I'll end it on my own bed.*

With numbed heart and hands, I managed to swallow

every pill in my possession, washing them all down with the wine. *I suppose I should say goodbye to someone, though.*

Before losing consciousness, I dialed a drugging buddy. I knew he was out partying, so I left a message on his machine at home. *This is safe enough, because by the time he hears it, I'll be long gone.*

"I just want to say goodbye, Sean. I've decided I just can't go on with life. It's nobody's fault. Please believe me. It's nobody's fault. Goodbye, my friend."

ตรตรตร

What on earth? This can't be hell, and it sure isn't heaven. I struggled into wakefulness, and the first thing I saw was Andrew's brown eyes, brimming and full of pain.

"Why, Kayla?"

"I'm not supposed to be here," I protested. "I know I took enough pills to do me in."

"Why?" he repeated.

"Life has no meaning. My brother's dead. My family thinks I'm a loser. I'm nothing but a piece of shit. You and I aren't together. I can't kick the drugs or booze. It's not your fault. I just wanted out." I struggled to sit.

"So, why am I *not* out?" I crossed my arms and glared. "Sean was at the bar …"

"I know," Andrew interrupted. "He told me."

"That's why I called *him*. I knew he'd hear the message *after* I was dead."

"Well, he had some sort of premonition and came home. As soon as he heard the message, he called the sheriff. They broke down your door and found you unconscious, so they called the paramedics who took you to emergency. Then the hospital had you transferred to this place. They handle drug addictions and suicidal patients here."

I sagged against the bed. *I can't even do suicide right.* "So, now what?"

"They want to release you today," Andrew told me a short time later.

"No." I shook my head. "I need help. I want to go to a rehab place for further treatment."

I joined AA after my release from the first of many rehab centers. There, I learned that I was powerless to help myself. I needed to seek God's help and find people to hold me accountable. I worked my way through the 12-step program and finally achieved some form of sanity in my life.

Meanwhile, I knew Andrew still struggled with his own alcoholic demons, so I invited him to attend AA with me, but he refused.

"I'm happy it's working for you, really I am," Andrew told me later, "but I feel I need something more. You know I've been going to a new church — GTaustin — and I feel I can get what I need there."

"Go for it, then, but organized religion isn't for me."

~~~

I knew Andrew had turned his life over to Jesus, whatever that meant, and once again he invited me to go to church with him.

"Come to GTaustin. You'll love it. They're not dull. They're quite lively."

I guess I can go just once. After all, Andrew was willing to come to AA with me.

"I'll go."

These people are loony, I thought as I sat through the worship time. *People jumping all over the place and clapping and waving hands. And they think I have a problem? Catholics are much more sedate.*

"Do you accept Jesus?" the pastor's wife asked me after the service.

"Sure. The same way I accept Buddha and Hari Krishna and Muhammad."

"He's different."

"Yeah, right."

"I don't think this is for me," I told Andrew.

"I'll respect your decision," he said, "but Jesus is real. His power is real. Have you noticed that he delivered me from alcohol?"

"Well, now that you mention it, I haven't heard about you drinking lately. What happened?"

"Do you remember when I got back from that business trip in September?"

"When I called and knew you were totally wasted?"

"Yes. I admitted to you then that I knew my drinking was completely out of control."

"And I insisted again that you go to AA with me. You agreed, but the next day you refused again. You said you were going to take a break from drinking. How could you manage it without any outside help?"

"I didn't manage it on my own," Andrew replied. "You and I both know how impossible that would be. I got a text message from a lady at GTaustin asking me to come to church that Sunday and that she'd save a seat for me."

"So what happened?"

"I admitted to Jesus that I was allowing alcohol to control my life, and so I tried to make a deal with God. I said, 'If you will help me stop drinking, I will not drink again for 90 days. I will take a break until New Year's Eve.'"

"So, did you?"

"I left church thinking, *I now have this under control because Jesus is on my side.* I think Jesus just snickered and said, 'Not good enough.' That Monday night on my way home from work, I decided to stop into the local sports bar and have a couple of beers. When I walked into that bar, every seat was taken in the bar and restaurant. There wasn't even standing room available at the bar. I turned around, walked out, drove home and went to sleep."

"Without touching a drop?" I could hardly believe what Andrew was telling me. He had always drunk so much more than me.

"How is this possible after all your years of hard drinking?"

"Two nights later I went to the church's weekly prayer service. While there, I broke down again and gave my heart and life to Jesus. I also told him that I just didn't want to stop drinking for three months but for the rest of my life. I prayed to Jesus and told him I was not strong enough to do this by myself and that I could only do it if he would help me. I promised to walk down whatever path he sent me on." Andrew's tone softened.

"It worked, Kayla. I haven't had a drink since, *and* all desire for alcohol disappeared as well. God is so good!"

I mulled over what Andrew had told me and remembered some fellow AA members who said they knew Jesus.

"I'd like to get to know that guy," I'd told them.

"Then, come to our Bible study," Justin said.

"I think I will."

❧❧❧

I'd been learning the truth about Jesus, not the hippy-dippy preconceptions I'd held for years. But, still, I felt worn out and down. *I've tried to make sense of my life through booze and drugs. I even tried to check out through suicide.*

"Jesus, if you're real, I need to know you are here. I need to see you." My body sagged onto the solid firmness of the floor. "I've tried everything else, so I may as well surrender to you. Everything I've tried has failed." I pressed my face deeper into the carpet. "I feel like I've been a chameleon all my life. I don't even know who I really am. I want you to make me the girl *you* created me to be."

ॐॐॐ

"Will you come back just one more time to GTaustin?" Andrew asked, six years after our separation.

I sighed. "I'll go, but I'll have to leave early for work."

"Remember that I took over the Romanian mission work? I had a fantastic time, and our pastor asked me to share about it next Sunday."

"Okay. I think I can handle that. I'll come."

We met in the church lobby. Pictures of children waiting for sponsors were scattered across a table.

"What is this?" I asked Andrew.

"Kids that I'm trying to get sponsorships for to help with their education. This is what I'm speaking about today to the congregation."

I sat in amazement listening to Andrew's talk. *Who is this man? The Andrew I know is so quiet, introverted, and here he is chatting like everyone in the congregation is an old friend. Amazing!* Then several revelations dawned in my mind and heart. *God, he is so precious. He's become a wonderful and humble person since you took over his life.* I felt a physical shift as my heart filled with love for this special man. *Send him a good woman to love him as he deserves to be loved.*

What about you? It seemed God spoke deep inside me.

Me? Are you serious?

Maybe you should find out.

"Andrew." My hands and voice shook as I faced him in the parking lot after the service. We were both in tears. "I am so proud of you."

I spent the next few weeks mulling over those words. *What about you?* I wondered, *Is this a man I can grow old with?* I couldn't stop thinking about him. For me, the answer was yes, but what about Andrew? Would he even want me?

I dialed the phone with shaking fingers and took a deep breath. "I get this feeling that you and I should be together again. Is that crazy, or what?"

There was a long silence. I imagined his eyes turned the color of warm chocolate brownies and a slow smile spread across his face.

"It's all I've ever wanted."

❧❧❧

GTaustin welcomed me with genuine love and acceptance. Nobody cared about my past failures — except me. I knew the people had prayed long and hard for me to come into a real relationship with Jesus, and all rejoiced at my presence. Pastor Kermit went out of his way to make me feel welcome every time I went. And Sandy, a greeter at the church, always took time to hug me, compliment me and encourage my walk with Jesus.

If they really, really knew, they'd despise me.
You know that's a lie, God said.
I knew, but the doubt remained.

In mid-October, I accepted an invitation to a two-day women's retreat. Rhonda, our bus driver, failed to flinch when I mentioned a few details of my past. Old thoughts of shame and worthlessness continued dogging me.

When we arrived at the center, I chose a bunk away from the other ladies. However, another woman named Carrie claimed the top for herself.

She doesn't like me, I thought, turning away before I could witness any disapproval.

What's this? I wondered when I returned to my bunk later. A small card lay on my pillow.

I'm so delighted you came to the retreat, Carrie had written. I tried to filter through her loving, accepting words with my own thoughts of worthlessness.

I sat in the afternoon session on Saturday and tried to concentrate on the message.

Come outside, and spend some time with me.

Jesus, I'm sitting in a meeting at a retreat. It would be rude to walk out.

I want to spend some time alone with you. Come on out, and take a stroll with me around the lake.

I wandered around the retreat campgrounds and continued my silent dialogue with Jesus.

I've been following you for some time now, Jesus, but I still feel so unworthy. I need you to show yourself to me this weekend. Something so drastic that I'll know you are real and you are God.

A woman who pastored a church in New York stood to speak that evening.

"God has a plan for you. He knows all about you — where you've been and where you are today. He knows every triumph and heartbreak. He knows all your successes and failures.

"My mom died giving birth to me. Alcoholics raised me. I was sexually molested and became both an alcoholic and a heroin addict myself. God took me off the streets. He was and is the only being with enough power to do so."

All around the room, women began weeping as her story resonated with their own. I felt no need to cry, even though our stories were so similar. When the meeting ended, I returned, dry-eyed, to the cabin.

That night I dreamed I saw a huge dump truck with a mechanical arm. I began dumping all my sins into the truck. As soon as it filled, the arm flung all the dirt into an abyss of nothingness. Again I filled the truck, and again the arm flung the sins to the vast unknown.

I'd had a Christian sponsor in AA, and I'd confided to her that I never felt good enough. As soon as Jesus gave me something wonderful, I felt I had to work to pay him back. I never felt I deserved the love of Jesus, no matter how many messages I heard to the contrary, nor how many worship songs proclaimed it.

I couldn't shake the oppressive feeling of

unworthiness, started in my early years when my siblings called me a bad child. Then, I began my own destructive lifestyle. Every bad thing that happened to me I felt I deserved. I never asked God, "Why me?" because I thought, "Of course I deserve this, so why not me?" Even after I had accepted the forgiving power of Jesus, I held his love at arm's length.

But in my dream, as I saw all my sins being flung into nothingness, my heart swelled with love and more love. Gratitude penetrated my understanding. I was worthy because *God* said I was worthy. Nothing more. Nothing less.

I slipped into a deep, healing sleep, and while my cabin mates awakened, dressed and packed for home, I slept on.

They must've gone for breakfast. I scanned the empty cabin and noticed the suitcases parked by the door. *At least I won't have to fight for the shower!*

I dressed and packed my own bag. Then, I headed to the dining hall, already emptied.

You are all alone here because nobody loves you, my doubts whispered in my ear. *Nobody wants to be with you. You deserve to be alone.*

I ran into Maria, the pastor who'd given the talk the night before. We were both in the ladies room just before the morning meeting started. I told her how similar our stories were and how I felt I'd never been good enough to satisfy my family or God.

"I've heard of an experiment," Maria said, "where a man addressed a body of water. Every day, he went out and cursed it. Soon, ice formed over it. Then, he switched and began to speak words of love to it. The water thawed and flowed again."

"That's interesting," I said.

"It's an analogy of your heart, Kayla. Humans are 60 percent water. The heart is 73 percent water. If you speak hate into your life, your heart will freeze over. If you speak love — Jesus' love — you will flow in his warmth and forgiveness."

All the verbal criticism from my siblings had formed ice over my heart. Only Jesus could make it flow again. "Thank you, Maria. I'll remember that."

I walked into the sanctuary, and to my surprise, Maria stood up to talk. "I feel the Holy Spirit is telling me to scrap what I had prepared and to tell you about an experiment involving water."

As she retold the event, I began bawling like a baby. Suddenly, the young lady behind me tapped me on the shoulder. I turned, and she handed me a folded note.

I opened it and read:

God wants <u>you</u> to know that you are <u>enough</u>!!!

I cried harder, bent over with deepening sobs. These precious people were helping to melt the ice around my heart. After a while, I turned to the girl. "How did you know?"

"I didn't," she said. "I only wrote what God told me to

write. He says you are beautiful, and he loves you just as you are and — you are enough."

Later, when the ladies took communion, I split my morsel of bread and handed a piece to the young lady. She did the same. We shared in the body of Christ.

For the first time, I understood what Jesus meant when he gave his followers bread and said, "This is my body." And the cup of wine saying, "This is my blood of the covenant, which is poured out for many for the forgiveness of sins" (Matthew 26:26, 28).

I felt overwhelmed by an avalanche of God's love. God's pure, accepting, all-encompassing love.

I am loved. I am loved. I am loved. Tears of shame turned to cleansing ones as my heart began singing.

> "You turned my wailing into dancing;
> you removed my sackcloth and clothed me with joy,
> that my heart may sing your praises and not be silent.
> LORD my God, I will praise you forever."
> (Psalm 30:11-12)

"Kayla, I'd like to invite you to a small dinner party," Carrie said, shortly after our return from the retreat. "Will you come?"

I nodded, but my heart raced. *Whatever will I do? I used to need a whole bottle of wine to gain enough courage to face strangers. What if they judge me? What if they don't like me?*

I skipped the bottle and went to the dinner with a

prayer for God's strength on my lips. The dear ladies surrounded me with authentic, loving energy, as pure as their personalities. I reveled in the freedom to love and be loved, saturated in their acceptance of me as *me*.

Everything I ever sought in life — love, acceptance, confidence — and had used alcohol and drugs to find, I finally found in Jesus and at GTaustin. Jesus healed me of my addictions, and the people of GTaustin became my visible representation of his love.

I found myself feeling spoiled by God. I felt special — handpicked. And deeply loved.

SNAKE SKIN
The Story of Thomas
Written by Christian Simon

Do as I say, not as I do. These aren't the exact words of my father, but the adage certainly captures his message.

What did he mean to tell me? Don't drink as much as I do. Don't yell at your mother or at any woman. *Just please don't make my mistakes, Thomas.*

It's good advice. The only problem is that I should have never worried about his mistakes.

I should have worried about my own.

የየ

"She tried to kill me with a belt."

This is what Lauren told me when she hurried to get into my car.

She meant her mother. Her *mother* tried to kill her.

I racked my brain for the right thing to say but came up empty. Nobody ever told me something like that before.

Not thinking and just doing, I hit the lock button and put the car into drive, but before we could move forward, Lauren's mother stepped in front of the car. She was manic, screaming so loudly. Turning to Lauren, I wanted to ask her what was going on, but my mind froze and instinct took over.

Regaining control, I slammed the car into reverse and backed away, creating distance between Lauren's mom and us. Making a three-point turn, I steered the car toward the curb and stepped on the gas. As I stole glances in the rearview mirror, I saw Lauren's mother's body contort in anger, her figure shrinking more and more until she became a small dot and then was finally gone.

"What is going on?" I asked Lauren as soon as we got away from her house.

"She's on something again. Thank you for picking me up."

This part wasn't new. Her mom used drugs, and Lauren always suffered for it. As I placed my hand on Lauren's, I thought about the apartment I lived in as a child. It wasn't too far from Lauren's mother's house. Maybe the guy who sold her mom the drugs was a kid I grew up with. It wouldn't surprise me. Some things were cyclical.

As we drove out of the neighborhood, we passed hundreds of apartments identical to Lauren's mother's — grey and white and stacked on top of each other like monochromatic Legos, surrounded by trash and graffiti, short streets and long streets. Outside the windshield, I saw young men hanging around, all draped in the same color, which served as both a welcome and a warning. The same kind of men who sat outside my house when I was a kid and would occasionally deliver brown bags with silver barrels jutting out the openings.

The sight was familiar.

Once when I was 7 or 8, I was walking back from my friend's when one of these men approached me. I could see his shadow slide out in front of me moments before I heard him yell.

"What're you doing here?" he boomed.

"I ... I," was all I could muster.

He moved closer, his eyes no different than how Lauren's mother's looked —focused, but empty. I braced myself for the worst, arms paralyzed at my sides. I was completely aware that his massive arms could easily break my own. As I stood there, waiting for what would come next, I felt the blood drain from my arms and then my chest and stomach. I felt so light, like I was nothing. I thought that if I was lucky, I might just float away.

But seconds passed, and nothing happened. In fact, I only felt a caress, and then I heard, "Come on, baby."

When I looked up, I saw an older woman, her face worried but determined. She guided me away, and I hurried to my apartment door. When I looked back, I saw the man kick her butt like she was a dog.

"Lauren," I said, forcing myself back into the present, "you're all right. I'm getting you out of here."

After arriving at my friend Dan's, I decided to stay there with Lauren for the night. Dan was more than okay with this because he had been close with both Lauren and me since she and I first started dating. In fact, he was the one who introduced us.

Dan had met Lauren's friend Ashley outside of a Walmart over the summer a few years before. She was wearing short shorts and caught his eye as we were leaving the store. Then we saw her again at a gas station near the store. They exchanged numbers, and a few weeks later, Dan, Ashley, Lauren and I were all hanging out on what she began to call "our first double date."

It's funny how love actually begins. You don't find too many people who fell for each other over anonymous love letters or had their first date canoeing through a swan-filled lake. For some of us, it begins at an Exxon Mobil and a Walmart parking lot.

But sitting there that night, looking at Lauren, I knew I wouldn't have it any other way. I thought she looked different there at Dan's, but she always did. She would change her makeup, her clothes or her hair. Sometimes she would even walk differently. But she would always act the same — extroverted and outgoing. She never made me chase her. She made it known from the beginning that she and I would be involved, on any level, no matter what I had to say about the matter.

That was just Lauren.

జౕజౕజౕ

When I woke the next morning, I left Dan's house and drove out to the suburbs of Austin. It was warm out, and the day seemed brighter than usual. I loved the early mornings on weekends, before the roads filled with traffic. I drove in silence, alone with my thoughts as I watched the early sun soften the city.

I often thought about my grandfather. *Do as I do, not as I say.* This would have been his adage. He was more like a compass than a rulebook, always recalibrating, always finding the right way, or at least the way he believed to be right. He was quiet in his later years when he was living in our home. There weren't ever discussions of morality or lessons of what to do and what not to do. Instead, there were Sunday mornings at church, where I would watch him help anyone in any way he could. He would greet people and listen to them — genuinely caring about what they said.

Throughout the actual sermons, while I was bored out of my mind, kicking the chair in front of me, my grandfather would listen closely to the pastor, occasionally patting me on the shoulder to redirect my attention. It didn't matter that the speaker might have been boring or that the message was familiar. He was interested in something beyond the delivery. He saw truth in it all.

I looked out of my car window and into suburbia, wondering what my grandfather would think of me and if he would understand who I had become. I remembered how old he looked, even back then, when I was a child. My mother told me he worked on railroads when he lived in Mexico. His hands were tough — calloused and chewed up from the intensive labor of his trade. I'd always thought that he was made of different stuff than me, shaped by experiences and wisdom I didn't understand.

After driving deep into the suburbs, I parked outside a house that sat front and center on a wide street. The neighboring homes looked identical, all of them with manicured lawns that shimmered in the same freshly mowed pattern. The houses themselves were stucco and big, like they fit entire, complete families — mothers and fathers, two kids and a dog. They had front yards and backyards where the fathers probably played catch with their sons before the mothers came outside to yell "Dinner!" An entirely different world than where I grew up. That part of the city looked as if one day thousands of families just packed up and left to start a new way of life.

As I waited in the car, not wanting to be early, I turned on some music. The bass thudded softly from my speakers as I turned the dial on my radio. The noise was gravelly, almost static, but this only enhanced the music's gritty quality. Then, catching the beat on the run, the rapper's voice came across the speakers low and fluid. I grinned as I thought about the confidence he demonstrated as he entered the song. He knew he was good.

This is what I am, I thought. This rapper, a poet, really, was no different than I — he knew what it was like to be successful. Seek pleasure where you can find it. I wondered what else there could be.

Checking the time, I turned off the engine and the music. Before I left my car, I checked my face and hair in the mirror, crinkling my brow and tightening my lips while I assessed myself. My long braids and loose-fitting T-shirt looked foreign in this neighborhood, like when a weatherman in a suit stands against a green screen displaying a smiling sun or a cartoon field. But I felt good just being there. I could feel it in my bones. Especially considering what had happened the night before and everything that was going on with Lauren, from her mom to the fights we'd been having. Sitting in that neighborhood, all of the trouble seemed to belong to another person's life. This place had become where I escaped all that.

I left my car and walked to the house after I deemed myself presentable. I smoothed my hair into place one last time and then rang the doorbell. When the door opened, I took a deep breath and smiled at the girl standing in the doorway. She was beautiful. Her skin was a smooth mixture of light and dark. Her eyes were green, or hazel, and when the sunlight caught them they looked gold, like sweet tea or dusk in the summertime.

"Hi. My parents are in the family room," she said, freezing me to the porch with her smile.

"You look beautiful, Rachel," I fumbled.

Taking me by the hand, Rachel walked me inside where family portraits and framed memories hung on the wall. As we walked through the hallway and into the family room, I could see her parents sitting on the sofa.

"Hi, Thomas, how are you?" her mother asked after hearing us walk into the room. Her face looked kind, just like her daughter's.

"Never been better," I replied, stooping down to kiss her daughter on the cheek.

పాపాపా

When my father drank, my mother argued. She loudly vented her feelings about him coming home drunk. I would go into my room and play my music — listening to lyrics telling me not to care, to numb myself with another life, one with more pleasure and less caring. I could still hear my parents screaming over the sound of my music, but the noise inside my headphones drowned their words enough for me to mask the harsh things being said. The sounds of their shouts would soon fade into a background noise that matched that of the music in my mind. I could escape into a different world — one that was safe because it was detached from mothers and fathers. It was a world about things that couldn't yell back. Things that could be attained and then controlled.

Money, cars, women. *Especially women.*

Sometimes, I'd look out of my window and down into the world below. The men, the ones who would occasionally hand each other the bags of guns or money, were always there in groups, talking through clouds of smoke. They were like actors living out the words — *the code of bravado* — that I was listening to in my music. I would wonder where their parents were and if they were fighting and screaming inside a different apartment — the dad drunk, the mom standing up to him.

Mom did take me to church, though. She used to drop me off for Sunday school. I'd sneak away to the store, always slipping back in time to meet her for the worship service. Mom raised me to know about God and faith from a young age, sharing her views on morals and values from the Bible. But as I grew older, I started to drift further away from God.

Many of my friends turned to drugs or gangs. Not me. Women became my vice. My relationships took up most of my time, and my life revolved around them.

Women pursued me, and I did nothing to discourage them. I enjoyed their pursuit and didn't blink at managing multiple relationships at once. If that meant I ended up being unfaithful, well, I figured that was just part of my life.

I still went to church, but if anyone there had known how promiscuous I was, he would have thought I didn't know anything about God, that I had turned my back on him.

❧❧❧

We spent the day together, and when we finished dinner that evening, Rachel picked up our dishes and carried them to the sink. As if on cue, her mother jumped to her feet.

"Let me help you, honey," she said, leaving the table to join Rachel in the other room. After her mother left, Rachel's father turned to me and smiled, shifting his body toward mine, as if to say, *You have my full attention, son.*

"I hear you've studied at San Antonio." He grinned and played with the tablecloth.

"Yes. Yes, I did. I also work at the Department of Public Safety."

"That's good. I bet law enforcement could use you. Strong, smart, knowledgeable about the city."

"I think so." I chuckled.

"I bet you do. You're a good guy, Thomas. I appreciate how you treat Rachel, too."

His last words hit me hard. Her parents loved their daughter so much that they had welcomed me without hesitation. I could almost see my grandfather shake his head in disapproval. But I pushed him out of my mind. His image, my conscience, was a barrier to what I needed from my relationship with Rachel. Besides, she had pursued me, no different than Lauren. If she wanted me, then she would take me like this. Any feeling of deceit or sorrow I felt as her father spoke so kindly to me was also pushed to the back of my mind.

I am not my grandfather, I thought.

ରେ ରେ ରେ

In high school, I never took alcohol or drugs too far. I heeded my father's advice and recognized what "too much" looked like. Success in high school meant staying out of trouble and receiving good enough grades to get into college. This is what the school faculty and my parents told me. What they didn't say was not to sleep with too many women. This never entered the conversation. Maybe it was due to embarrassment or the fact that an admissions board won't look into how many times you've woken up next to a different woman or hooked up with a girl whose name you can't remember. Besides, romancing women was fun. It felt good and didn't mean anything. Not to me at least.

I didn't begin to understand what having sex, let alone an entire relationship, meant to the women involved. This is what the teachers and my parents didn't explain to me. They didn't tell me that my habit, my desire to find pleasure with whatever woman I could, might just cut someone else down, which in turn would slowly destroy me.

അഅ

After I left Rachel's that night, I headed back to Dan's to see Lauren. She was exhausted from all the recent fights with her mom, so she was sound asleep. I sat and looked at her, wondering what she did that day and what she was thinking, if she was dreaming or if her mind was blank — her memory emptied in self-defense. Quietly, I took off my shoes and slid into bed next to her. Once under the sheets, I started to think about Rachel. I thought about how easy it was with her family. They had the house, the cars, everything money could buy. Dating Rachel was entering a new life — one with high ceilings and wood floors, married parents and nice cars.

For some time I lay awake in the darkness, not so much wondering whether what I was doing was right or wrong, just trying to reconcile if I actually cared or not. Then, coming from somewhere in the darkness, the familiar marimba sound of my phone began echoing throughout the room. Slipping out of the bed sheets, I fumbled for my phone, the catchy jazz tune sounding more like a cadenced screech. When I finally reached it, I could hear Lauren shift her body around while she woke.

"Babe," she said, "who's calling you this late?"

"A friend," I responded, without missing a beat.

"It's close to 2 a.m. What could *he* want?"

Looking at my phone to double-check the time, I glanced at the missed call notice displayed across my phone — *Rachel Franks*.

"I don't know what he wants," I said.

"What *who* wants?"

"Robert."

The dark room made it impossible for me to see Lauren, or for her to see me, but I stared in her direction, anyway, listening for some kind of sign of distress, maybe a body movement or even a sigh.

But there was nothing. Just fuzzy darkness and a deep silence.

Then, finally: "Let's go to bed, Thomas."

As I sat awake in bed, I knew that Lauren suspected the phone call was from a girl. Lauren wasn't stupid. She was just tired. Tired of asking who the other person was on the end of the line. Tired of accusations. It didn't take very long for intuition to become a choice: Stay and live with it or leave. Lauren had made her decision long before, and sleeping next to her that night, I knew she wouldn't leave. Lauren and I had our problems, no different than a lot of couples, but she wanted us to work. She cared for me and by not asking more about that call, or any of the other calls she knew were far too late to be normal, was somehow trying to protect us.

ॐॐॐ

I could never convince myself that I was not my father. I resisted the anger and destructive nature of alcoholism, but the force behind it all seemed to emerge in my own relationships with women before I recognized it. But even when I was arguing with Lauren, fuming beyond comprehension, I never blamed my father because the blame was not actually with him. I had my role, and I knew I needed to own it if I wanted the cycle to stop. So I turned to the last place I wanted to go — God. It was what my grandfather would have done. I understood that there might not be any answers for some time, but that if I waited and trusted in him, I could get square with myself and maybe Lauren.

When I first started to work at the Department of Public Safety, I'd been looking for a change. The other employees and the officers provided me with a different situation than what I had with my old friends. They seemed to have found some kind of truth regarding happiness — productivity. This seemed to be anything but a solution at first. It made my life monotonous, devoid of the meaning I had asked God for. There were days where I would sit under the glare of a fluorescent light, stacking and flipping through an endlessly replenishing pile of papers like a modern-day Sisyphus, wondering if my job was actually a punishment. But I trusted that what God gave me at that moment was what I needed, even if I didn't like or understand my place.

After a couple months at the department, I started to exercise after work. The gym became an outlet, and I enjoyed workouts with a friend and co-worker. His name was Mark, and I could tell he was different than the other guys in the gym. We lived separate lives outside of the facilities at the DPS, which is why it was surprising when he asked me one day whether I wanted to join him at church.

"What're you up to this weekend, bud?" he asked, supporting my elbows while I lifted a weight above my head.

"Nothing, man. What's up?" I threw the weights to the ground, gasping.

"You should come to church with me sometime."

I hauled a weight up and over my head and began lifting it repeatedly, buying time, trying to navigate my way to an answer.

"Sure," I finally said. "It's been a while, though, man. Do I need to wear anything special, or …?"

"Just come in whatever, man, it won't matter. Don't over think it. Just be there."

As we racked the weights and prepared to head out of the gym, I turned to Mark, wanting to thank him. He didn't understand how much the invitation meant. I had been so removed from church, I had no idea how to get back in. I felt like it didn't belong to me, that maybe I didn't deserve to go because of who I was, or rather, who I had become.

"I'll be there," I replied.

On the following Sunday, Lauren and I decided to go to Mark's church. When we entered the church, I immediately felt out of place. The church building looked like it could be a giant conference room during the week and a church on the weekend. The crowd of people wore suits or dresses and sat in rows of straight chairs. Despite the appealing, lively atmosphere in the auditorium, the formal attire I saw made me feel self-conscious and nervous. When we finally found Mark, Lauren and I rushed to say hi, eagerly trying to escape the gaze of the crowd.

"Hey, buddy," Mark whispered when I sat down next to him.

"Hey, what's up, man?" I replied quickly, adjusting my jeans and my shirt, making sure they looked in order.

Mark pointed to a few empty seats, then returned to his own in the front row.

Soon after we sat, a woman took the stage and started speaking. She introduced herself with the same last name as Mark. *Could she be his mom?* I wondered.

Later, she mentioned her son, glancing over at Mark. *Wow,* I thought. *He's the pastor's son! No wonder he's so different from the other guys.*

I was nervous throughout her entire sermon,

wondering if I should even be there. Hearing her speak about how God would forgive me, regardless of what I'd done, shook me. The actual person I was hurting and sleeping with was there with me, while I was being told that I could be forgiven. I wanted to scream out to Mark's mother and ask her how — how could I just move on from everything?

I had heard this message in church before, often with my grandfather as a child, without understanding or experience. It was one that always left me anxious when I was younger. I felt it was the people around me, pastors included, who pressured me to pray to God and ask for his forgiveness. But as Mark's mother asked the audience to pray to God that day, I felt different — I felt alone. I didn't have my mom or my grandfather by my side, and all the people around me began to fade into the background. I felt pressured to pray something. Yet, I felt like the pressure was not from anyone around me, but from inside me and maybe from God. The pastor, the people, the whole church seemed like a conduit for something else, so I decided to pray and ask God what he wanted out of my life.

God, please. I want more than this from my life. I surrender. Take control.

࿇࿇࿇

After attending Mark's church, my relationship with Rachel ended abruptly and with unmistakable finality, like at the end of a movie when the screen cuts to black before you are ready to stop watching. After recommitting my life, I knew I needed to end things with Rachel or with Lauren, but I couldn't bring myself to do it. I stopped sleeping with them both because I believed it was right in the eyes of God and that it would save them some embarrassment and pain. But I guess God couldn't wait for me to decide. He must have had other plans.

I was asleep on Rachel's sofa one day when I woke to the sound of the TV. Then I heard Rachel's voice come from the next room. As I walked to where she was talking, I heard Lauren's voice crackling through the receiver. I could only hear Rachel's words with clarity, but they were enough for me to understand.

When Rachel hung up, I didn't even try to make an excuse. I'd never left my cell phone unattended before. Not with Rachel, not with Lauren. But that day I did. For some reason, I left it near a table in a different room, too tired to think about keeping secrets. I had known, even before that moment, there was a possibility they might find out.

Rachel and I didn't speak much on the way out to my car. We didn't even discuss where to go to talk. We both just knew we needed to step outside so her parents wouldn't hear. Before I left, I turned to her mom and dad and smiled, wishing I could say something, but knowing it would be wrong.

"Why?" she asked when we were in my car.

"I'm sorry," I said, and I really was.

"You need to make a choice. Me or her. I haven't given up. You just need to make your choice."

You, Rachel. This was what I wanted to say. *You* and *Lauren.* But I couldn't, even if it was what I wanted. She didn't want to leave me, and I thought, for a fleeting moment, that I could still have them both. But I felt I had to do the right thing, even if it meant leaving Rachel and losing everything a relationship with her represented.

"I'll leave now," I said finally.

"So her," she said, her voice barely a whisper.

࿊࿊࿊

Lauren took the pain differently than Rachel. She had suspected I was communicating with other girls. The phone call confirmed the worst of those fears. But she was hiding something of her own. Lauren told me that she had been sleeping with other men. It broke me down to hear it. I'm not sure if she did it for revenge or pleasure or if there was even a reason at all. I thought back to the phone calls when Lauren almost found out about Rachel. I wondered if her phone was ringing, too, and I just didn't hear it.

Lauren and I began attending a church named GTaustin — the same one I had attended regularly as a child. I didn't skip out on Sunday school this time. Still, it was different than Mark's.

After attending, we found ourselves wanting to return. They accepted Lauren and me from the moment we entered the building. We had both been devastated by our actions, but when we attended GTaustin, I could feel the love of God through everyone around me. These people knew pain and seemed to understand the complexities of what we were experiencing. There weren't glares, and there wasn't tension. It felt like a place where we could deal with our past and create a future.

One Sunday, the pastor asked for people to come to the front of the church to pray and let go of anything that was holding them back. I felt like God was talking directly to me, saying, *Thomas, it's time to* really *surrender.*

I felt so broken. I believed God knew everything I had done, and yet he still forgave me. He even knew what I'd do before I did it, yet he chose me to be part of his family.

I walked to the front of the church and fell on my knees, crying. It was such an intense moment of really feeling connected to God. I prayed, "I surrender, God. Take control."

And that time, I meant it.

In the months that followed, I prayed a lot. I prayed over and over that God would give me a purpose. Lauren and I attended many special church events and conferences. Repeatedly, people took me aside and said they felt strongly that God wanted me to be involved in music.

Their words surprised me. I had never done anything musical before. But after I heard the same thing from so many people, I figured God might be trying to tell me something. I chose to believe God and ran with it. I started writing music. Rap music.

At first, I did it because it was a way to be productive. Music took my mind off the specifics — who Lauren had been with and, more painfully, why she had needed to be with someone else in the first place. She was probably asking herself the same questions. But I couldn't blame Lauren because I was just as guilty. Instead, I wanted to find a way to love her, regardless of what had happened.

As Lauren and I became more involved with the church, we found that we could give our past a different life, one that was outside our own, in the form of music. She sang on the worship team, and my music started to become something greater than I could have ever expected. While writing some lyrics to a song one afternoon, I thought back to a Bible verse I had recently read: "And we know that in all things God works for the good of those who love him, who have been called according to his purpose" (Romans 8:28).

Lauren and I wanted our relationship to honor God. We made the decision to stay celibate — to keep our relationship at a level we could handle and be proud of in God's eyes. We wanted to know each other on a level outside of sex. The desire was still there. Lauren was beautiful, and I felt more comfortable with her than with anyone else in the world. I loved to go to concerts or trips to the coast on the weekends with her, but I also spent my evenings with Lauren at the gym or on a couch. She was my best friend — someone who looked over my music when I needed help, wanting to support my interests while also allowing me to participate in her interests and experiences. I didn't want anything else. Just her. By putting our trust in God, we resisted the temptation of a sexual relationship for the next year and a half. We both believed only God had the power to help us do something like that.

I had once been that kid — angry, upset, looking for the things my favorite music artists told me I needed in order to be happy. I started to wonder how I could help others avoid following the same path. I knew how good it looked and how easy it was to have the women, to tell the lies and to live life like it was a music video, devoid of actual meaning. I never thought my mistakes could be a part of something that could help others, but I began to understand that they must be. They were exactly the reason.

During one of my performances, I rapped about consumption and pleasure — the things I'd fought so hard to conquer. I challenged the young men in the audience to question what society and our culture told them about being a man.

"Strength," I told them, "isn't sleeping with random women or being able to destroy someone else. Strength is being nailed to a cross and then forgiving the men who did it. Strength is carrying the pain of a world on your broken shoulders while you were spit on. That is strength. That is a man — the same one who is my God and has the power to forgive me so that Lauren and I could forgive one another. Being a man is being in love — with God and the people you care for."

After I finished speaking, I left the stage and a man approached me. "God is going to use you to do great things for other people, I know it."

"Thank you," I replied, not sure what to make of his comment.

I was taken aback by this man because I didn't ask God to be great. I just asked to be forgiven. But this man wasn't the only one to tell me something like this. The more events I did, more and more people would come up to me and tell me they were grateful for what I was telling kids who came out to hear me. I recognized that God was giving me an opportunity for redemption, and I didn't hesitate to take it.

❧❧❧

Lauren and I married after we became involved at GTaustin. After our wedding, we began to make trips to the beach to watch the sunrise. Once we were there, we would watch the water turn from black to red, like slow-moving magma erupting from beneath the waves. At night, we would get in our sleeping bags and look out of our tent and into the sky. Cold wind would occasionally sweep across our faces, and Lauren would move closer to me to keep warm.

It wasn't difficult to find God in nature, to look out at the waves and feel cared for. It was an entire world created for us, beautiful but complex. Lauren and I loved to walk down to the rock formations near the edge of the water and watch the ripples move over the sand and wash it clean. I felt God's presence on these trips, speaking to me through small moments of peace, and I thanked him for that.

As I looked back at all that God had given me, I knew that I wanted this kind of happiness for other young men and women who grew up like I did. My life was so much clearer after trusting God to take control.

I just needed to crawl out of myself, out from my old skin, and start over new.

CONCLUSION

Now that you have read their stories, you no doubt see that their life change was not about a certain strategy or method. It's about a person, the person of Jesus Christ. He came to this earth, lived and died in order for us to be changed, transformed.

Every time we see another changed life, it increases our awareness that Jesus really loves people and he is actively seeking to change lives. Think about it: How did you get this book? We believe you read this book because God brought it to you seeking to reveal his love to you.

Whether you're a man or a woman, single or married, an engineer or a laborer, a parent or a student, we believe God came to save you. He came to save all of us from the hellish pain we've wallowed in and to offer real joy and the opportunity to share in real life that will last forever through faith in Jesus Christ.

Do you have honest questions that such radical change is possible? It seems too good to be true, doesn't it? Each of us at GTaustin warmly invites you to come and check out our church family. Freely ask questions, examine our statements, see if we're "for real" and, if you choose, journey with us at whatever pace you are comfortable. You will find that we are far from perfect. Our scars and sometimes open wounds are still healing, but we just want you to know God is still completing the process of authentic life change in us. We still make mistakes in our journey, like everyone will.

Therefore, we acknowledge our continued need for each other's forgiveness and support. We need the love of God just as much as we did the day before we believed in him.

How does this change occur? In 2 Corinthians, chapter 5, in the New Living Translation of the Bible, we read: "At one time we thought of Christ merely from a human point of view. How differently we know him now! This means that anyone who belongs to Christ has become a new person. **The old life is gone; a new life has begun.**"

"So where do I start?" you may be asking. First, recognize that what you're doing isn't working. Accept the fact that Jesus desires to forgive you for your bad decisions and selfish motives. Realize that without this forgiveness, you will continue a life separated from God and his amazing love. In the Bible, the book of Romans, chapter 6, verse 23 tells us that the result of sin (seeking our way rather than God's way) is death, but the gift that God freely gives is everlasting life found in Jesus Christ.

In Romans 10:9-10, God tells us what to do to allow him to begin the change process in our lives. "If you confess with your mouth that Jesus is Lord and believe in your heart that God raised him from the dead, you will be saved. For it is by believing in your heart that you are made right with God, and it is by confessing with your mouth that you are saved."

So, that is what God says you must do to be saved and begin to be changed — nothing more — simply believe and confess.

Why not pray now?

Lord Jesus, my choices have not resulted in the happiness I hoped they would bring. Not only have I experienced pain, I've also caused it. I know I am separated from you, but I want that to change. I am sorry for the choices I've made that have hurt myself and others and denied you. I believe your death paid for my sins, and you are now alive to change me from the inside out. Would you please do that now? I ask you to come and live in me so that I can sense you are here with me. Thank you for hearing and changing me. Now please help me know when you are speaking to me, so I can cooperate with your efforts to change me. Amen.

Austin's unfolding story of God's love is still being written — and your name is in it. I invite you to come and let us celebrate God's work in your life! I hope to see you this Sunday!

Blessings,
Pastor Kermit Bell
Senior Pastor
GTaustin

We would love for you to join us at one of our campuses!

North Campus
Sundays @ 10am
Current: Parkside Elementary | 301 Garner Park Dr
Future: 15841 Ronald Reagan Blvd | Leander, TX | 78641

Central Campus
Sundays @ 8:30 & 10:30am
2700 Northland Dr | Austin, TX | 78756

Manor Campus
Sundays @ 11am
18201 Blake Manor Rd | Manor, TX | 78653

South Campus (Spanish)
Sundays @ 10:30am
8902 Bluff Springs Road | Austin, TX | 78744

Contact Information
Phone: 512.459.5481
Website: gtaustin.com
Email: info@gtaustin.com
Facebook: www.facebook.com/gtaustin.ag

For more information on reaching your city with stories from your church, go to www.testimonybooks.com.

GOOD CATCH PUBLISHING